Tackling Child Abuse

WQEIC
The George Thompson Library
Please return the book on or before the last date shown below

WITHDRAWN

** A fine is payable for each overdue book **

Lisa Firth

KT-514-333

Independence

Wyggeston QE I
WITHDRAWN

00494039

First published by Independence
The Studio, High Green
Great Shelford
Cambridge CB22 5EG
England

© Independence 2009

Copyright
This book is sold subject to the condition that it shall not,
by way of trade or otherwise, be lent, resold, hired out or otherwise
circulated in any form of binding or cover other than that in which it
is published without the publisher's prior consent.

Photocopy licence
The material in this book is protected by copyright. However, the
purchaser is free to make multiple copies of particular articles for instructional
purposes for immediate use within the purchasing institution.
Making copies of the entire book is not permitted.

British Library Cataloguing in Publication Data
Tackling Child Abuse – (Issues; v.179)
1. Child abuse
I. Series II. Firth, Lisa
362.7'6-dc22

ISBN 978 1 86168 503 2

Printed in Great Britain
MWL Print Group Ltd

Cover
The illustration on the front cover is by
Don Hatcher.

CONTENTS

Chapter One: Child Abuse

Chapter Two: Sexual Abuse

Chapter Three: Discipline and Abuse

Acc. No.

00494039

Class No.

362.76 FiR

Useful information for readers

Dear Reader,

Issues: Tackling Child Abuse

No child should have to live in fear, but as the Baby P case recently demonstrated, abuse is a tragic reality for some children – experts have estimated that up to one child in ten is abused in the UK. These children may suffer neglect, emotional, physical or sexual abuse, in many cases from those responsible for their care. This title examines the issue of child abuse and how it can be tackled. It also looks at the debate about smacking.

The purpose of *Issues*

Tackling Child Abuse is the one hundred and seventy-ninth volume in the **Issues** series. The aim of this series is to offer up-to-date information about important issues in our world. Whether you are a regular reader or new to the series, we do hope you find this book a useful overview of the many and complex issues involved in the topic. This title replaces an older volume in the **Issues** series, Volume 132: **Child Abuse** which is now out of print.

Titles in the **Issues** series are resource books designed to be of especial use to those undertaking project work or requiring an overview of facts, opinions and information on a particular subject, particularly as a prelude to undertaking their own research.

The information in this book is not from a single author, publication or organisation; the value of this unique series lies in the fact that it presents information from a wide variety of sources, including:

⇨ Government reports and statistics
⇨ Newspaper articles and features
⇨ Information from think-tanks and policy institutes
⇨ Magazine features and surveys
⇨ Website material
⇨ Literature from lobby groups and charitable organisations.*

Critical evaluation

Because the information reprinted here is from a number of different sources, readers should bear in mind the origin of the text and whether the source is likely to have a particular bias or agenda when presenting information (just as they would if undertaking their own research). It is hoped that, as you read about the many aspects of the issues explored in this book, you will critically evaluate the information presented. It is important that you decide whether you are being presented with facts or opinions. Does the writer give a biased or an unbiased report? If an opinion is being expressed, do you agree with the writer?

Tackling Child Abuse offers a useful starting point for those who need convenient access to information about the many issues involved. However, it is only a starting point. Following each article is a URL to the relevant organisation's website, which you may wish to visit for further information.

Kind regards,

Lisa Firth
Editor, **Issues** series

** Please note that Independence Publishers has no political affiliations or opinions on the topics covered in the **Issues** series, and any views quoted in this book are not necessarily those of the publisher or its staff.*

ISSUES TODAY
A RESOURCE FOR KEY STAGE 3

Younger readers can also benefit from the thorough editorial process which characterises the **Issues** series with our resource books for 11- to 14-year-old students, **Issues Today**. In addition to containing information from a wide range of sources, rewritten with this age group in mind, **Issues Today** titles also feature comprehensive glossaries, an accessible and attractive layout and handy tasks and assignments which can be used in class, for homework or as a revision aid. In addition, these titles are fully photocopiable. For more information, please visit our website (www.independence. co.uk).

Wyggeston QE1 College
Library

What is child abuse?

Information from Young Scot

Growing up can be difficult. But even when they feel bad, most children and young people know that they're loved and cared for. But not everyone gets that love and care, or gets it as often as they need it. Sometimes young people get hurt or used by adults or other young people, and that can mean they are being abused.

Abuse can mean a lot of different things – it's not always easy to know if you or someone you know is being abused. But the important thing to remember is that no-one has the right to hurt you or make you do anything that feels wrong.

If you or someone you know is being abused in any way, then the most important thing to do is speak out – tell someone about it. You don't have to hide it.

Neglect

Neglect is when you are not being looked after or supervised properly. If the people who look after you don't give you the important things you need, or make it hard for you to take care of yourself. You could be suffering from neglect if:

⇨ you don't have enough warm clothes;

⇨ you don't have enough to eat and drink;

⇨ you're left alone, or left in charge of family without adult help;

⇨ you're forced to sleep somewhere cold or uncomfortable;

⇨ no-one helps you when you're ill or you've been hurt.

If this is happening to you, you might think that it's your fault. It isn't.

No-one has the right to neglect you. If you speak out about neglect, there are people who care – they will listen to you and help you.

Emotional abuse

Emotional abuse is when someone tries to make you feel bad. This can be saying things on purpose to scare you, or putting you down or humiliating you. If someone is always telling you that you're ugly, or fat, or stupid or that they wish you'd never been born, that's emotional abuse.

If this is happening to you, you might think that it's your fault. It isn't. No-one has the right to emotionally abuse you. If you speak out about it, there are people who care – they will listen to you and help you.

Sexual abuse

Sexual abuse can happen to anyone – boys or girls. The chances are that it will never happen to you, but if it does, you're not alone. Sexual abuse is when:

⇨ you're touched in a way you don't like;

⇨ you're being forced to have sex;

⇨ you're forced to look at sexual pictures or videos;

⇨ you're made to do something sexual that feels uncomfortable or wrong.

If this is happening to you, you might think that it's your fault. It isn't. No-one has the right to sexually abuse you. If you speak out about it, there are people who care – they will listen to you and help you.

Help = ChildLine

If you want to speak to someone you can call ChildLine: 0800 1111.

When you phone ChildLine, you'll be able to speak to someone who cares about your problems. The counsellors are all trained – they will listen to you and try to help you.

If you're scared or feel out of control, that's OK. You can tell them. It's their job to listen to you and put you in touch with someone who can make it stop.

Speaking out about abuse can be really difficult, but it's the right thing to do. Think about how you'll feel when the abuse has stopped.

All calls to ChildLine are completely confidential – you can talk about whatever you want to and we won't tell anyone else, unless you want us to.

Your ChildLine counsellor will only take action if they feel it's an emergency. ChildLine is always open – call 0800 1111 anytime. Lines can sometimes be busy, but please keep trying and someone will answer.

⇨ The above information is reprinted with kind permission from Young Scot. Visit www.youngscot.org for more information.

© Young Scot

Child abuse

This article tells you what you can do about child abuse, who you can report it to, and what might happen if you do

What is child abuse?

Child abuse is when someone is ill-treating a child, causing damage to the child's health or personal development. A child can be suffering abuse if they:

⇨ have been physically injured;
⇨ are suffering from sexual abuse;
⇨ are suffering from emotional abuse;
⇨ are being neglected.

Neglecting a child

You are neglecting a child if you fail to take care of them properly, for example, by failing to protect them from danger, cold or starvation. This does not have to be deliberate. You can also be neglecting a child if you give them very little affection or attention. A child who fails to grow properly might also be seen as having been neglected.

You might be neglecting a child if you leave them alone at home. This does not depend on the age of a child but on the circumstances and whether the child is at risk of being badly harmed.

Reporting child abuse

If you are worried that a child is being abused and want to report it to someone, there are lots of people you can talk to.

Reporting child abuse to social services

When you report child abuse to social services, they must look into it if they think there is a real risk to the safety or well-being of the child. Social services will decide if the child needs protection and what needs to be done to protect them. If, after initial enquiries, they decide that the child is not at risk, no further action may be taken.

Their enquiries could last several weeks, and may involve several interviews, family visits or medical examinations. Social services will interview the child, and may also interview anyone the child has come into contact with. Usually, social services will tell a child's parents that they are making enquiries.

However, in some cases, they may start making their enquiries before they let the parents know.

In cases of serious abuse, and in all cases of sexual abuse, social services will tell the police. Occasionally, social services will take urgent action to have the child removed from the family home and placed under police protection.

Once they have made enquiries and consulted with others, social services may decide further action is needed. There are a number of recommendations they can make, including:

⇨ police investigation;
⇨ applying for a court order for permission to place the child in care;
⇨ applying for a court order to place the child under the supervision of the local authority or a probation officer. This means the family will get help and support for the child to stay at home;
⇨ placing the child's name on the child protection register.

Social services don't often recommend court action or criminal prosecution, but this will depend on the circumstances.

Child protection register

A child will be placed on the child protection register if social services thinks there is a risk they will be badly harmed. A plan will be drawn up to protect the child and provide support to the child's family. The plan may involve an agreement with the child's parents to place the child in care. This could be with a foster family, in a children's home or a residential school.

> ### A child will be placed on the child protection register if social services thinks there is a risk they will be badly harmed

Reporting child abuse to the National Society for the Prevention of Cruelty to Children (NSPCC)

You can report child abuse to the NSPCC. The NSPCC runs a confidential freephone helpline for

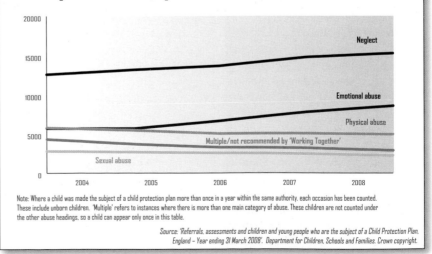

Children subject of a Child Protection Plan

Children who became the subject of a Child Protection Plan (CPP), by category of abuse. Years ending 31 March 2004 to 2008, England.

Note: Where a child was made the subject of a child protection plan more than once in a year within the same authority, each occasion has been counted. These include unborn children. 'Multiple' refers to instances where there is more than one main category of abuse. These children are not counted under the other abuse headings, so a child can appear only once in this table.

Source: 'Referrals, assessments and children and young people who are the subject of a Child Protection Plan, England – Year ending 31 March 2008'. Department for Children, Schools and Families. Crown copyright.

anyone who wants to report child abuse (see under Further help for contact details). When you speak to the helpline, you do not have to give your personal details if you don't want to. If you do give your details, the NSPCC may have to pass these on to social services, or the police, but will ask them not to pass your details onto the person or family you have concerns about.

If you report concerns about child abuse to the NSPCC, they must do something about it.

If you report concerns about child abuse to the NSPCC, they must do something about it

Reporting child abuse to the police

If you report child abuse to the police, they must, by law, investigate. If the child is under 16, they will usually involve social services.

In some emergency circumstances, the police can remove a child from home and take them into 'police protection' for up to 72 hours. They don't have to go to court to get permission for this.

As a result of police investigations, legal action may be taken against the child abuser. If the abuser is taken to court and found guilty, they will be punished and may be prevented from abusing others in the future. However, there is no guarantee that they will be found guilty.

The abuse victim may have to give evidence in court, which could be extremely upsetting. However, support is available for witnesses and, in some circumstances, the victim may not have to appear in court in person but will be able to give evidence via video or live television links.

Other people you can report child abuse to

You can also report concerns about child abuse to a number of other people including: health visitors; doctors and hospital staff; youth and community workers; probation officers; teachers and other school staff; nursery staff; education welfare officers; educational psychologists.

You should be aware that these people may have to pass on your concerns to social services or the police.

Rehousing because of child abuse

If you are looking after a child who is being abused, you could ask your local authority housing department to help with rehousing. However, if you do this, the local authority may make enquiries about the abuse, even if you don't want them to. Depending on the circumstances your local authority may be able to rehouse your family, rehouse the abuser, or rehouse the abuse victim.

There are also a number of legal measures you could take to prevent the abuser from staying in their home. If you want to do this, you should get legal advice.

If you are the mother or father of a child who is being abused, and you are suffering from domestic violence, you may be able to move to a refuge or get emergency accommodation from the local authority. If you are in this situation, you should get help from an advice agency – see under Further help at the end of this article.

Children suffering abuse

If you are a child suffering from abuse, you can get help by talking to the NSPCC or Childline (see under Further help).

You may also need to get urgent medical help, for example, to deal with injuries, pregnancy testing, emergency contraception or HIV tests. You can get medical help from your GP, the accident and emergency department of your local hospital or a family planning clinic such as the Brook Advisory Centre – see under Further help.

If you are under 16 and a health professional suspects you are being abused, they must report it to the police, social services or NSPCC, even if you don't want them to.

In some cases, it may be possible to claim financial compensation for being abused. You can get advice from an advice agency about this – see under Further help.

Further help

Citizens Advice Bureaux

Citizens Advice Bureaux give free, confidential, impartial and independent advice to help you solve problems. To find your nearest CAB, including those that give advice by e-mail, click on 'nearest CAB' on the Citizens Advice website, or look under C in your phone book. In some circumstances, your CAB may have to pass on details of child abuse to social services or the police.

NSPCC

Helpline: 0808 800 5000
E-mail: help@nspcc.org.uk
Website: www.nspcc.org.uk

Childline

Helpline: 0800 1111
Freepost address: Freepost, NATN 1111, London E1 6BR
Website: www.childline.org.uk

All calls to Childline are treated confidentially, but if Childline suspects danger or a threat to life, they will contact social services or the police. They will tell the child that confidentiality has been broken.

Brook Advisory Centres

Tel: 020 7284 6040 (information on nearest centre)
Helpline: 0800 018 5023
E-mail: admin@brookcentres.org.uk
Website: www.brook.org.uk

This information is produced by Citizens Advice, an operating name of The National Association of Citizens Advice Bureaux. It is intended to provide general information only and should not be taken as a full statement of the law. The information applies to England and Wales only.

This information was last updated on 1 September 2009, and is reviewed on a monthly basis. If it is some time since you obtained this information, please contact your local Citizens Advice Bureau to check if it is still correct. Or visit our website – www.adviceguide.org.uk – where you can download an up-to-date copy.

1 September 2009

⇨ The above information is reprinted with kind permission from Citizens Advice. Visit www.adviceguide.org.uk for more information on this and many more topics.

© *Citizens Advice*

One in ten children suffer abuse, say experts

By Sarah Boseley,
Health Editor

The true scale of the maltreatment of children in the UK is revealed by child abuse experts today who say that one in ten suffers physical, sexual, emotional abuse or neglect.

Unlike Baby P, who died in Haringey, north London, while on the at-risk register after months of abuse and neglect, most maltreated children are not even referred to the authorities.

Teachers, GPs and paediatricians have no confidence in the ability of social services to make a difference to their lives and fear the child's plight will be made worse if he or she is taken into care and placed in a foster family, they say.

A series of papers published today by the *Lancet* medical journal in collaboration with the Royal College of Paediatrics and Child Health paints a grim picture of the unseen sufferings of an estimated one million children a year in the UK.

Between 4% and 16% of children suffer physical abuse, such as hitting, punching, beating and burning, according to a paper by Ruth Gilbert and colleagues from University College London's Institute of Child Health. The figures come from research in high-income countries, including the UK, which is not thought to differ from the average.

Some 5-10% of girls and 1-5% of boys have been subjected to penetrative sex, usually by a family friend or relative. If sexual abuse is defined more widely - as anything from being shown pornographic magazines to rape - it is estimated that it will include at least 15% of girls and 5% of boys.

Around 10% of children suffer emotional abuse every year, the paper says, which includes persistently being made to feel worthless, unwanted or scared. More still - up to 15% a year - suffer neglect, defined as the failure of their parents or carers to meet the child's basic emotional or physical needs or ensure their safety.

Those like Baby P who are picked up by the social services and placed on the at-risk register are only the tip of the iceberg. The plight of fewer than one in ten maltreated children is investigated and substantiated by child protection services.

The experts underline a key finding from the case of Baby P - that professionals are not communicating and sharing their suspicions.

Lancet editor Richard Horton said the findings, which had taken a year to reach publication, had 'huge significance for considering an appropriate and measured response to the findings around Baby P'.

He added: 'What this report does emphasise is the extent of the risk factors and consequences of child maltreatment, which are of such complexity that any reflex attempt to apportion blame or think there is a simple solution to this issue is to completely misrepresent the extent and depth of the problem.'

The papers also expose the paucity of evidence behind the decisions taken by health professionals and social workers. Far more research is needed into finding out what will prevent a child being abused. 'We don't know how effective existing practice is,' said Jane Barlow, professor of public health in the early years at Warwick University, co-author of the paper on interventions. 'These are some of the most vulnerable children out there in society.'

In a *Lancet* commentary, Dr Horton says the series 'will unfortunately not halt the blight of child abuse, because the phenomenon is too common, too surreptitious and too deeply rooted in deprivation and other social ills - but we nonetheless hope to raise awareness of the scientific evidence that is available, and indeed essential, to guide paediatricians and other professionals in their practice with children who might have been abused and to help bring a new logic and clarity to public debate about this contentious area.'

3 December 2008

© *Guardian News & Media Ltd 2008*

Child abuse – signs and symptoms

Information from Kidscape

Although these signs do not necessarily indicate that a child has been abused, they may help adults recognise that something is wrong. The possibility of abuse should be investigated if a child shows a number of these symptoms, or any of them to a marked degree:

Sexual abuse

⇨ Being overly affectionate or knowledgeable in a sexual way inappropriate to the child's age;
⇨ Medical problems such as chronic itching, pain in the genitals, venereal diseases;
⇨ Other extreme reactions, such as depression, self-mutilation, suicide attempts, running away, overdoses, anorexia;
⇨ Personality changes such as becoming insecure or clinging;
⇨ Regressing to younger behaviour patterns such as thumb sucking or bringing out discarded cuddly toys;
⇨ Sudden loss of appetite or compulsive eating;
⇨ Being isolated or withdrawn;
⇨ Inability to concentrate;
⇨ Lack of trust or fear of someone they know well, such as not

wanting to be alone with a babysitter or child minder;
⇨ Starting to wet again, day or night/nightmares;
⇨ Become worried about clothing being removed;
⇨ Suddenly drawing sexually explicit pictures;
⇨ Trying to be 'ultra-good' or perfect; overreacting to criticism.

Physical abuse

⇨ Unexplained recurrent injuries or burns;
⇨ Improbable excuses or refusal to explain injuries;
⇨ Wearing clothes to cover injuries, even in hot weather;
⇨ Refusal to undress for gym;
⇨ Bald patches;
⇨ Chronic running away;
⇨ Fear of medical help or examination;
⇨ Self-destructive tendencies;
⇨ Aggression towards others;

⇨ Fear of physical contact – shrinking back if touched;
⇨ Admitting that they are punished, but the punishment is excessive (such as a child being beaten every night to 'make him study');
⇨ Fear of suspected abuser being contacted.

Emotional abuse

⇨ Physical, mental and emotional development lags;
⇨ Sudden speech disorders;
⇨ Continual self-depreciation ('I'm stupid, ugly, worthless, etc');
⇨ Overreaction to mistakes;
⇨ Extreme fear of any new situation;
⇨ Inappropriate response to pain ('I deserve this');
⇨ Neurotic behaviour (rocking, hair twisting, self-mutilation);
⇨ Extremes of passivity or aggression.

Neglect

⇨ Constant hunger;
⇨ Poor personal hygiene;
⇨ Constant tiredness;
⇨ Poor state of clothing;
⇨ Emaciation;
⇨ Untreated medical problems;
⇨ No social relationships;
⇨ Compulsive scavenging;
⇨ Destructive tendencies.

Note: A child may be subjected to a combination of different kinds of abuse.

It is also possible that a child may show no outward signs and hide what is happening from everyone.

Suspected abuse

If you suspect that a child is being abused, seek advice from the police or social services. It is preferable that you identify yourself and give details. However, if you feel unsure and would like to discuss the situation, ring the National Society for the Prevention of Cruelty to Children (NSPCC) Helpline, or the Royal Scottish

Society for the Prevention of Cruelty to Children, or the Irish Society for the Prevention of Cruelty to Children. You can speak to these organisations (and the police and social services) anonymously. The numbers are given on the Kidscape website, www.kidscape.org.uk.

Knowing how damaging abuse is to children, it is up to the adults around them to take responsibility for stopping it.

If a child tells you about abuse:
⇨ Stay calm and be reassuring;
⇨ Find a quiet place to talk;
⇨ Believe in what you are being told;
⇨ Listen, but do not press for information;
⇨ Say that you are glad that the child told you;
⇨ If it will help the child to cope, say that the abuser has a problem;
⇨ Say that you will do your best to protect and support the child;
⇨ If necessary, seek medical help and contact the police or social services;
⇨ If your child has told another adult, such as a teacher or school nurse,

contact them. Their advice may make it easier to help your child;
⇨ Determine if this incident may affect how your child reacts at school. It may be advisable to liaise with you child's teacher, school nurse or headteacher;
⇨ Acknowledge that your child may have angry, sad or even guilty feelings about what happened, but stress that the abuse was not the child's fault. Acknowledge that you will probably need help dealing with your own feelings;
⇨ Seek counselling for yourself and your child through the organisations listed on the Kidscape website.

Where to get help
You may consider using the school as a resource, as the staff should have a network of agencies they work with, and be able to give you advice.

You can contact official agencies or self-help groups. If you are concerned about what action may be taken, ask before you proceed.

The following can be contacted through your telephone directory:
⇨ Police;
⇨ Social Services;
⇨ Samaritans (0345 909090);
⇨ National Society for the Prevention of Cruelty to Children (NSPCC) in England, Wales and Northern Ireland (Freephone 0800 800 500);
⇨ Children First 0131 337 8539;
⇨ Irish Society for the Prevention of Cruelty to Children (ISPCC) (00 353 742 9744);
⇨ ChildLine (0800 1111);
⇨ Parentline (0808 800 2222).

For a free copy of the leaflet *Why My Child?* which helps parents deal with the sexual abuse of their child, send a large SAE marked 'Why My Child?' with two loose first class stamps to:
Kidscape
2 Grosvenor Gardens
London SW1W ODH
Tel: 020 7730 3300
You can order the leaflets at www.kidscape.org.uk/shop or you can email us for more details at webinfo@kidscape.org.uk

⇨ The above information is reprinted with kind permission from Kidscape. Visit www.kidscape.org.uk for more information.

© Kidscape

Definitions of child maltreatment

Terminology	Definition	Comment
Child maltreatment*	Any act of commission or omission by a parent or other caregiver that results in harm, potential for harm, or threat of harm to a child. Harm does not need to be intended	In the USA, 82% of substantiated cases were perpetrated by parents or other caregivers
Physical abuse*	Intentional use of physical force *or implements* against a child that results in, or has the potential to result in, physical injury	Includes hitting, kicking, punching, beating, stabbing, biting, pushing, shoving, throwing, pulling, dragging, shaking, strangling, smothering, burning, scalding, and poisoning. 77% of perpetrators were parents according to US figures for substantiated physical abuse
Sexual abuse*	Any completed or attempted sexual act, sexual contact, or non-contact sexual interaction with a child by a caregiver**	Penetration: between mouth, penis, vulva or anus of the child and another individual. Contact: intentional touching directly or through clothing of genitalia, buttocks or breasts (excluding contact required for normal care). Non-contact: exposure to sexual activity, filming or prostitution. For substantiated cases in the USA in 2006, 26% of perpetrators were parents and 29% a relative other than a parent. Parents form a smaller percentage (3-5%) of perpetrators of self-reported sexual abuse
Psychological (or emotional) abuse*	Intentional behaviour that conveys to a child that he/she is worthless, flawed, unloved, unwanted, endangered, or valued only in meeting another's needs. *In the UK, the definition includes harmful parent-child interactions which are unintentional: 'the persistent emotional ill-treatment of a child such as to cause severe and persistent adverse effects on the child's emotional development'*	Can be continual or episodic – e.g. triggered by substance misuse. Can include blaming, belittling, degrading, intimidating, terrorising, isolating, or otherwise behaving in a manner that is harmful, potentially harmful, or insensitive to the child's developmental needs, or can potentially damage the child psychologically or emotionally. Witnessing intimate-partner violence can be classified as exposure to psychological abuse. 81% of substantiated cases in the USA were perpetrated by parents
Neglect*	Failure to meet a child's basic physical, emotional, medical/dental, or educational needs; failure to provide adequate nutrition, hygiene, or shelter; or failure to ensure a child's safety	Includes failure to provide adequate food, clothing, or accommodation; not seeking medical attention when needed; allowing a child to miss large amounts of school; and failure to protect a child from violence in the home or neighbourhood or from avoidable hazards. Parents make up 87% of substantiated cases in the USA
Intimate-partner violence	Any incident of threatening behaviour, violence, or abuse (psychological, physical, sexual, financial, or emotional) between adults who are, or have been, intimate partners or family members, irrespective of sex or sexuality	Most frequently the perpetrator is the man in heterosexual couples, but there is growing recognition of violence inflicted by women. One community survey reported unanimous agreement that punching, slapping, or forcing a partner to have sex should be regarded as intimate-partner violence, but there was less consensus about emotional or economic abuse

*Definitions are based on Centers for Disease Control and Prevention report 2008, with modifications in italics.
**Includes substitute caregivers in a temporary custodial role (e.g. teachers, coaches, clergy, and relatives)

Reprinted from 'The Lancet', Vol 373, Ruth Gilbert, Cathy Spatz Widom, Kevin Browne, David Fergusson, Elspeth Webb, Staffan Janson. Burden and consequences of child maltreatment in high-income countries. Page 69. Copyright (2009), with permission from Elsevier.

People 'too afraid' to report child neglect concerns

Information from Action for Children

One in four adults (25%) have been worried that a child they know or living in their area is being neglected, and over a third (38%) did not tell anyone about their concerns, a new survey published by Action for Children reveals today.

The survey has been commissioned to highlight the difficulty of identifying and preventing the neglect of children. Neglect involves a wide range of complex factors from children feeling that they are not loved, nourished, supported and clothed, to worrying that their home is not safe and secure. Action for Children's experience of working with thousands of the most vulnerable families across the UK has provided the charity with further evidence on the issue of neglect and the practical, long-term solutions that combat it.

One in four adults (25%) have been worried that a child they know or living in their area is being neglected, and over a third (38%) did not tell anyone about their concerns

It comes as child neglect is becoming an ever-growing safe-guarding concern. In 2008 in England alone neglect was the reason why 45% of children were on the child protection register, compared to 15% for physical abuse, 7% for sexual abuse and 25% for emotional abuse.

The survey polled over 1,000 adults and parents in the UK and highlighted the public's lack of understanding

action for children

of child neglect and the reasons why adults hesitate to act on their suspicions. The results include:

⇨ 16% of adults said they did not tell anyone because they were frightened of repercussions or it may cause them trouble;

⇨ 15% said they did not tell anyone because it was not any of their business;

⇨ One in ten of adults (11%) would tell a neighbour, relative or friend about their suspicions first rather than social services or the police;

⇨ 15% said that a lack of proof prevented them from doing anything;

⇨ 23% said they did not think they had enough information about who to ask for help.

Action for Children warns that public confusion and misunderstanding around child neglect means that services may not find out about families where children are at risk at an early enough stage to prevent serious harm to children. Neglect can be harder to recognise than other forms of child abuse because it is often a symptom of other long-term and complex problems in a family rather than an easily recognisable one-off event. It can be hard for people around the family to know the right time to do something and feel comfortable and supported in acting on their instincts.

The charity is now launching a major piece of research to investigate how neglect should be tackled.

Announcing the survey findings, Clare Tickell, Chief Executive at Action for Children, says: 'Child neglect is a real danger to children and also often indicates underlying and serious problems in the family as a whole. In our child-centred services across the UK, Action for Children brings together a range of expert professionals, working alongside vulnerable families and we have learned that communities as a whole need to understand the effects on children of living in neglectful families. Today we're announcing the start of an investigation that will look at the most effective ways to intervene early in cases of neglect.'

Leading the research for Action for Children, Professor Tony Long at Salford University says; 'Unlike sexual or physical abuse, neglect is often overlooked and poorly understood. The results of this work between the University of Salford and Action for Children will inform Government policy, and have a major impact on the way children and their families are supported.'

Researchers will work with Action for Children services in Scotland, Wales and England looking at the reasons why families are referred for support, what needs and prob-lems they have, what support they are given and the long-term effects of this work on the children involved.

25 February 2009

⇨ The above information is reprinted with kind permission from Action for Children. Visit www.actionforchildren.org.uk for more information on this and other related topics.

© *Action for Children*

How the abuse industry is exploiting Baby P

If the killing of Baby P wasn't awful enough, now his death is being used to institute a new era of familial fear and spying

It is becoming clear that the death of Baby P was a double tragedy. First, there was the tragedy of the 17-month-old boy's neglect and death at the hands of his so-called carers in Haringey, London. Second, there is the tragedy of the 'lessons learned': that depraved abuse is widespread; that children around the UK are in mortal danger from their parents and guardians; and that social services must become more confident and cocky about removing children from the family home. One tragic death is being exploited to exaggerate, vastly, the scale of child abuse in the UK, and to re-empower the 'abuse industry' to interfere in family life.

> **One tragic death is being exploited to exaggerate, vastly, the scale of child abuse in the UK**

This week the respected medical journal *The Lancet* published an extensive series of articles on child abuse in Britain, which argues that abuse is far more prevalent than we think, but professionals are failing to spot it or take interventionist action. Though *The Lancet* has been working on the series for the past year, it has, upon its publication, become intimately bound up with the Baby P tragedy. 'One in ten children mistreated,' screamed newspaper headlines, next to now-familiar photographs of Baby P. The Baby P link-up isn't surprising, when you consider that *The Lancet* itself, in its press release for its series, upfronted the 'severe child abuse' of Baby P. There's nothing like a timely, tawdry death to promote one's research.

By Brendan O'Neill

The Lancet – whose series on child abuse contains four papers that run to 63 pages – argues that in affluent countries, including the UK, one in ten children (or ten per cent) suffer from abuse, yet only around one per cent of children are referred to child protection services. It also claims that 15 per cent of girls and five per cent of boys have been exposed to 'some sort of sexual abuse' by the age of 18, and, perhaps most alarmingly, that five to ten per cent of girls and one to five per cent of boys have suffered from penetrative sexual abuse. The image is of a nation in which very large numbers of children are being neglected, abused or even raped, yet where professionals are 'too timid' to take action. One contributor to *The Lancet* says we must do more to 'ensure we are taking children away from dangerous situations'.

However, these 'stats' are more a product of a low-down and prurient misanthropy than rigorous research. For all the declaratory headlines about 'widespread abuse' in the UK, *The Lancet* series is in fact based, not on scientific investigation of the occurrence of child abuse in Britain in 2008, but on a massive and unwieldy overview of more than 500 abuse studies carried out everywhere from the UK to New Zealand. *The Lancet* authors lumped the studies together – despite the fact that they study different things, and use vastly different methodologies – analysed them, and arrived at the conclusion that, all things considered, probably about ten per cent of children in wealthy countries are abused. Yet as one critic pointed out, some of the old studies are themselves unreliable, containing 'small numbers, unrepresentative samples and generalised conclusions'. The notion that you might marry the studies together, pool their wildly differing results, and come to a neat

conclusion about the number of kids being abused in the UK today is unadulterated hocus-pocus.

Indeed, so flaky and shaky is the figure of 'one in ten British children abused' that it doesn't even appear in *The Lancet* series itself. Instead, the authors gave this estimate of ten per cent at their press conference, perhaps recognising that they needed a neat figure to tantalise a press corps that was highly unlikely to wade through 63 pages of analysis of old analyses of child abuse everywhere from Haringey to Wellington. One reason why the authors might have arrived at such a high number of abuse cases is because they used a flabby, all-encompassing definition of abuse, borrowed from one of the American reports that they reanalysed: 'Child maltreatment encompasses any acts of commission or omission by a parent or other caregiver that result in harm, potential for harm, or threat of harm to a child even if harm is not the intended result.'

One reason why the authors might have arrived at such a high number of abuse cases is because they used a flabby, all-encompassing definition of abuse

---

This could involve almost anything. Indeed, for *The Lancet* physical abuse can mean 'hitting, punching, burning'. Parents who physically discipline their children 'with an implement' or through regular 'hitting' are lumped together with parents who stub cigarettes out on their children's bodies or who seriously assault them. This suggests that *The Lancet* doesn't understand what is and what is not an act of violence against a child. A parent who disciplines his or her child with an implement is not acting violently: the intention is not to injure or abuse, but to discipline; the motivation is mostly love or concern rather than malice. By equating corporal discipline (something that many

parents, especially of the traditionalist variety, still carry out) with wanton violence against children (which is thankfully rare), *The Lancet* study demonises certain parental practices and brackets even loving parents in the Baby P category.

The Lancet's working definition of abuse also includes psychological and emotional abuse, which can include 'behaviour that conveys to a child that they are worthless, flawed or unloved'. Again, this is an extremely broad definition. Stern or disciplinarian parents may make their children feel 'flawed' because they want them to improve and be successful – is that abuse? Other parents are not naturally touchy-feely and may not heap love on their children – does that make them guilty of some kind of 'emotional neglect'? Many of the studies analysed by *The Lancet* involved self-reporting of abuse or 'retrospective recollections' by adults, so there is also a strong subjective element here: teenagers and young adults often report feeling 'worthless' or 'unloved', but that doesn't necessarily mean that they are. Nobody benefits from creating a slippery slope from sternly criticising a child's flaws to seriously neglecting their emotional needs.

As an example of how unwieldy, and suspicious, is *The Lancet's* view of abuse, its authors argue that many professionals, such as teachers, do not realise that 'bad behaviour or arriving unwashed at school' may be the result of maltreatment. Here, we can see how almost anything can become an indicator of abuse. Yes, being unwashed might be a sign of maltreatment – but it might just as easily, and more probably, be a sign of an untidy household or of a child that dashes out in the morning without doing as his mum says and washing his hair. Bad behaviour can spring from abuse... but it can also spring from such perfectly ordinary things as childish mischievousness or a rebellious streak. When everything from stern discipline to burning and from criticising flaws to psychological neglect is defined as 'abuse', and when everything from being grubby behind the ears to naughty in class is taken as a potential indicator of neglect, it is

amazing that only 'one in ten' children falls into *The Lancet's* promiscuous at-risk category.

The category of sexual abuse seems ill-defined, too. As Stephen Glover said in the *Daily Mail*: 'Look at the wide range of figures. One to five per cent of boys are supposedly exposed to penetrative abuse. Which is it? You would think me pretty flaky if I said that London was a city of two to ten million people. The difference is huge.' Also, for the *Lancet* sexual abuse seems to include a vast array of unpleasant experiences for anyone aged under 18. Yet as the *Independent* argued: 'A girl of 17 who is pressed into having sex by a boyfriend, while a clear instance of abuse, is a different case from that of a seven-year-old raped by a relative... How helpful is it, and how meaningful, to gather the many varieties of cruelty meted out by adults to children – and by children to each other – into one catch-all category of child maltreatment?'

In the wake of Baby P, and the idea that social workers are not doing enough to uncover abuse, and now this new study that wildly claims abuse is occurring all over the place, many now argue that it is incumbent on all of us to become spies, lookouts for neglect and horror. Even if it gives rise to a 'culture of denunciation', says one columnist, aptly drawing upon Stalinist ideology, 'child abusers need to know on an intimate, cultural level that their actions will not be discreetly ignored'; we need more 'public intervention', apparently, to tackle the 'magnitude' of the child abuse problem. This, too, is a double tragedy. Ordinary families will become objects of suspicion; and if people's and officialdom's resources are directed towards spying on everything from tough discipline to lack of washing, all 'signs of abuse', then we may well miss the real and still rare cases of violence against children that occur in some communities.

4 December 2008

⇨ The above information is reprinted with kind permission from Spiked. Visit www.spiked-online.com for more information.

© Spiked

Neglected children should be taken from parents

It is not necessarily in the best interests of vulnerable children to leave them with their parents, says Martin Narey

By Martin Narey

I recently spent time with some remarkable Barnardo's staff who were working with mothers whose children had been taken into care. They were, on behalf of the local authority, assessing the mothers' competence and motivation to resume parental care. It was clear that the welfare of the child was the overwhelming consideration of my staff. But, nevertheless, the optimum solution was for natural parents and child to be reunited.

I heard of one family whose care had been scandalously neglectful. In foster care, the children were beginning to do well: their health had begun to improve and they were, for the first time in many months, attending school. But the whole direction of statutory and voluntary sector effort, it seemed, was directed at whether the family could be fixed. In time, that would probably involve the children returning to a home which might again descend into inadequacy and neglect. Why would we want to take that risk? Why would we expose a child to the possibility of further neglect?

One reason is that we despair of putting children in care. The philosophy is that we should do everything possible to deflect children from the dreadful consequences of being looked after. Regrettably I have contributed to that. Shortly after I arrived at Barnardo's from running the Prison and Probation Services, and after meeting so many prisoners who had been in care, I spoke scathingly about its inadequacy. Three years on, I regret having been so simplistic. I knew little of the challenges facing local authorities and I was yet to recognise the very high calibre and commitment of those who lead children's services. The predictable and opportunistic

castigation of the men and women dedicated to this task leaves me nauseous.

There were as many arguments for taking more children into care as there were for getting more children out of care

In fact my then, rather glib, dismissal of local authority effort matched the orthodoxy about children in care – that, particularly in the voluntary sector, being in care and more particularly being in residential as opposed to foster care, is always the worst possible choice.

In 1981 there were 92,000 children in care, two thirds of whom (58,000) were in orphanages. The cost of

caring for so many in that way was unsustainable and when a number of high profile abuse scandals brought these mammoth institutions into disrepute they began to close and the voluntary sector rapidly abandoned residential care. By March of 2008, there were many fewer children in care (about 64,000), and only ten per cent in residential homes. Such a transformation was a triumph.

Tasked by Beverley Hughes in 2007 to see whether we might further reduce the numbers in care, and despite being keen to do so, I found it hard to deliver. I was challenged by troubled social workers, who whispered to me in tones which suggested they were struggling with the guilt of heresy, that the best outcomes for many children would often be much speedier separation from inadequate parents followed by early adoption. Eventually I concluded that there were as many arguments for taking more children into care as there were for getting more children out of care.

It is important not to overreact in the aftermath of Baby P's tragic death,

the horror of Shannon Matthews's dreadful childhood or the recent concerns over Doncaster.

But I wonder whether we need to reassess our approach to care, and to residential care in particular. The orthodoxy that says that care is always to be avoided but that when it is resorted to, care needs to mean foster care, leaves me feeling very nervous.

I recently had lunch with some foster carers. They were remarkable people. But I fear that we sometimes pursue fostering long after it has ceased to be the best outcome in terms of stability. I met one carer who for two years has persisted with a young girl who – shamefully – had suffered 41 previous placements. What are we thinking of?

And on a visit to one of the handful of small homes Barnardo's still runs, I met an 11-year-old boy. On the autistic spectrum, and with challenging behaviour, he was beginning to thrive in a caring unit where there were enough staff to cope with him. But he was about to move to his 13th foster placement. Staff told me he might last six weeks; he lasted four. Yet again, he was too much for willing carers. Is such a case an exception? Certainly not.

We need to have an honest debate about the potential for residential care, not based on the failures of the past, but on the possibilities for the future. The reality is that when the wake of Baby P has disappeared we shall return to a status quo where social workers who intervene to remove children from parents face vilification. The emphasis is – too much in my view – on fixing families. Social workers cannot continue to be vilified when that fixing breaks down, sometimes tragically.

Martin Narey is chief executive of Barnardo's. This is an abridged version of an article to appear in the February 2009 issue of Public Policy Research, *the journal of the IPPR think tank.*
24 January 2009

© Telegraph Media Group Limited (2009)

Guidance to help identify child maltreatment

Information from NICE

NICE has today (22 July 2009) issued guidance to help healthcare professionals to identify children who may have been maltreated. The guidance provides a summary of alerting features that should prompt a healthcare professional to consider, suspect or exclude child maltreatment. Child maltreatment includes neglect, physical, sexual and emotional abuse, and fabricated or induced illness.

In the 12 months to 31 March 2008 there were 538,500 referrals of children to social services departments

In the 12 months to 31 March 2008 there were 538,500 referrals of children to social services departments (DCSF 2008). The number of referrals only represents those children identified as 'at risk' of maltreatment and as such is likely to underestimate the number of children being maltreated.

There is strong evidence of the harmful short- and long-term effects of child maltreatment. All aspects of the child's health, development and wellbeing can be affected and these effects can last into adulthood and include anxiety, depression, substance misuse, and self-destructive, oppositional or antisocial behaviours. In adulthood, there may be difficulties in forming or sustaining close relationships, sustaining employment and parenting capacity. Physical abuse may result in lifelong disability or physical scarring and harmful psychological consequences, and may even be fatal. The National Service Framework (NSF) for Children, Young People and Maternity Services for England states: 'The high cost of abuse and neglect both to individuals (and to society) underpins the duty on all agencies to be proactive in safeguarding children.'

This guidance provides a comprehensive summary of physical and psychological symptoms, signs and interactions, that may alert healthcare professionals to suspect maltreatment. This includes bruises, cuts, ano-genital signs and symptoms, neglect and emotional abuse observed in parent (or carer) child interactions. The guidance is intended to encourage healthcare professionals to think holistically when a child presents so that they think about what they see, hear and any other information they receive to help them build up a picture. For example, if maltreatment is considered, they may need to look at the whole child, gather relevant information from other sources and discuss the case with a senior colleague and review the child. The guidance will ensure that children who need help get it early in order to prevent further or future harm, and to enable additional supportive services to be provided to families where needed.

Dr Sheila Shribman, National Clinical Director, Children, Young People and Maternity Services said: 'Spotting the signs of child maltreatment and protecting vulnerable children is an important but often difficult challenge for healthcare professionals. I welcome this guidance as an important means of helping frontline staff identify maltreatment and provide support for them in taking appropriate action.'

Andrew Dillon, NICE Chief Executive, said: 'We want to give healthcare professionals the confidence to recognise the signs of maltreatment and to know when to refer on to a specialist. This guidance does not include recommendations on how to diagnose, confirm or disprove maltreatment; this should be done by specialists in social care, following Local Safeguarding Children Board procedures.'

Danya Glaser, Guideline Development Group Chair and Consultant Child and Adolescent Psychiatrist, said: 'Child maltreatment is a real problem but it may go unrecognised. It can include neglect and emotional abuse as well as sexual and physical abuse, and often has long-lasting effects into adulthood. Healthcare professionals can find it difficult to acknowledge and act on the signs of maltreatment and may be concerned that action may lead to more harm to the child or the relationship with the family. However, this should not preclude them from following the appropriate course of action to prevent further harm to the child. This guidance provides healthcare professionals with a comprehensive list of alerting features which will help them recognise child maltreatment as it happens. Parenting is difficult, parents often do not intend to harm their children and this guidance is also about identifying the parents who need more help to look after their children.'

Monica Lakhanpaul, Clinical Co-director, NCC for Women's and Children's Health, said: 'This guidance is a tool aimed to support front line health care professionals to take responsibility to ensure the safety of children and to ensure children and families receive help in a timely way. Health professionals need to be able to recognise clinical features that should alert them to gather further information about the child, discuss the child or share information with colleagues and decide whether a child may be being maltreated in any way or may have an alternative diagnosis. This guidance will help professionals to decide the urgency with which they need to involve other agencies or involve people with more expertise in the field.'

Healthcare professionals can find it difficult to acknowledge and act on the signs of maltreatment and may be concerned that action may lead to more harm to the child

---

Christine Habgood, GP, Brighton and Hove, said: 'This guideline provides welcome support for front-line healthcare professionals in their work with children. It gives them the information they need to identify those children who have been maltreated and need protection and help. Although most clinical encounters with children involve physical, behavioural or emotional issues, child maltreatment needs to be in the list of possible causes for many of these presentations. We are asking GPs and others to think really carefully about what they are seeing, to discuss their suspicions with other colleagues if necessary or refer children on to the appropriate agencies if they suspect them to be maltreated. Every child should feel safe and secure and we all need to make sure this happens.'

Kathryn Gutteridge, User Representative and Consultant Midwife, Sandwell and West Birmingham NHS Trust, said: 'Child abuse is a wide-reaching problem in society; particularly in the place they should feel safe – their own homes. The very people that children should be able to trust and seek comfort, respect and unconditional love from are more often than not the abuser in their lives. I am one of those adults who experienced the harm of sexual and emotional abuse – it made my life impossible at times and harder than it should ever have been. I grew up with unimaginable stressors and harm; this certainly affected my physical and emotional wellbeing into adulthood. Healthcare professionals could have helped me but they didn't, this guidance is a start for front-line healthcare workers to begin to identify the signs that children show when they are experiencing abuse.'
22 January 2009

⇨ National Institute for Health and Clinical Excellence (NICE) 2009. London: NICE. Also available at www.nice.org.uk Reproduced with permission.

© National Institute for Health and Clinical Excellence

RIGHTS OF THE CHILD

REPORTING ABUSE

LEGAL CONSEQUENCES

CORRECT DIAGNOSIS

DEALING WITH PHYSICAL AND PSYCHOLOGICAL ABUSE

PROFESSIONAL PEER SUPPORT

PREVENTING FURTHER HARM

CHILD'S WELFARE

Counselling for sexual abuse reaches new high

Information from the NSPCC

ChildLine counselled more children for sexual abuse last year than at any other time in its 22-year history. They included 465 children aged seven or under and nearly 6,000 of these calls related to rape.

In 2007/08 13,237 children were counselled for sexual abuse by ChildLine, the 24-hour confidential helpline for children and young people. This is up from 8,637 in 2004/05 – a 53 per cent increase over three years. During the same three-year period, the overall number of children counselled also rose but by only 26 per cent.

ChildLine counselled on average one child aged seven and under a day for sexual abuse during 2007/08

The increase meant that ChildLine counselled on average one child aged seven and under a day for sexual abuse during 2007/08. Most children counselled for sexual abuse – 61 per cent (6,681) – were aged 12 to 15 years.

Of the 13,237 children counselled for sexual abuse by ChildLine in 2007/08 the vast majority were abused by someone they knew:

⇨ 59 per cent said they had been sexually abused by a family member;

⇨ 29 per cent said they had been sexually abused by someone else known to them;

⇨ Four per cent said they had been sexually abused by a stranger;

⇨ 8,457 were girls (64 per cent);

⇨ 4,780 were boys (36 per cent).

Since ChildLine joined with the NSPCC three years ago, the NSPCC has enabled ChildLine to expand its service to try and meet the huge demand from young people, and now has more volunteer counsellors, more bases, and answers more calls than ever before. Nevertheless, ChildLine is still only able to answer two-thirds of the 2.3m calls it receives every year.

In response, the NSPCC is urgently calling on the public to donate to the charity's Child's Voice Appeal (www.childsvoiceappeal.org. uk), a three-year £50m fundraising campaign launched last year. The Appeal will help expand both ChildLine and the NSPCC Helpline – for adults concerned about the safety or welfare of a child.

This is needed in addition to £30m already pledged by the UK government, which recognises the importance of expanding the NSPCC's helpline services.

Head of ChildLine Sue Minto commented: 'Every day, ChildLine receives dozens of harrowing calls about sexual abuse from children, some of whom are very young indeed. Children phone to talk in confidence about suffering different kinds of sexual abuse, the vast majority of the abusers being people they know, either within their families, or the wider family circle. They dare not speak about it, or ask for help, for fear of the consequences. Many of them have been threatened or intimidated into silence.

'Some calls about sex abuse include details of other extreme forms of abuse like being hit, tied up, threatened with their life and being plied with drugs. Many are less severe but still devastating for the child.

'We believe children are calling ChildLine partly because of awareness campaigns targeted at children like the NSPCC "Don't Hide It" campaign. Child sex abuse storylines on programmes like *Eastenders* also encourage children to speak out.

'As a result, more children now understand what sexual abuse is and are increasingly willing to turn to ChildLine for help. More ChildLine counsellors over the last few years has also meant more children helped and this is reflected in these latest figures.'

ChildLine founder and President Esther Rantzen said: 'These tragic calls come from children who have found the courage to ring a ChildLine counsellor. Yet there are many children whose cries for help cannot be answered because ChildLine simply does not have enough resources to answer every call. Our nightmare is the child who plucks up the courage to ring, fails to get through, and never dares try again. Imagine the distress of a child who cannot get through to a counsellor before she is raped again that night.

'As a ChildLine counsellor, I have experienced first hand these heart-wrenching calls from children who feel utterly alone until they make the call; I know the hope we provide these children literally saves precious young lives.

'ChildLine counsellors provide in-depth counselling to children for a whole range of problems from physical or sexual abuse through to worries about exams, pregnancy and bullying. ChildLine is on hand 24 hours a day, seven days a week for any child whatever their problem. We therefore urgently need to expand the service so that every child's cry for help can be answered.'

People can help answer a child's cry for help by donating to the NSPCC's Child's Voice Appeal by visiting www.childsvoiceappeal.org.uk. Anyone worried about the welfare of a child can call the NSPCC helpline 0808 800 5000.

Notes to Editors

About the Child's Voice Appeal

The Child's Voice Appeal, which launched on 22 September 2008, aims to raise £50m so that the NSPCC's vital helplines can answer many more cries for help. To date the appeal has raised £13m.

The funds will mean that ChildLine's volunteers can counsel 500,000 more calls every year; children will be able to choose how they access Child-Line's help – by phone, online or by text; the NSPCC Helpline can grow by over 60 per cent to counsel 18,000 more adults a year who have concerns about a child; and counsellors can provide personalised help by email to nearly five times as many concerned adults.

The government has pledged £30m over four years towards the expansion of ChildLine and the NSPCC Helpline, but the NSPCC needs the support of the public to raise a further £50m through the Child's Voice Appeal, to make its vision a reality.

Everyone can support the Child's Voice Appeal at www.childsvoiceappeal.org.uk

About the NSPCC

The NSPCC is the UK's leading children charity specialising in child protection and the prevention of cruelty to children. The NSPCC's purpose is to end cruelty to children FULL STOP. Its vision is of a society where all children are loved, valued and able to fulfil their potential. The NSPCC runs 180 projects and services across the United Kingdom and Channel Islands, including ChildLine, the UK's free, confidential 24-hour helpline for children and young people. The NSPCC helps over 10,000 children and their families every year.

Calls to ChildLine about sexual abuse

All names and identifying details have been changed to protect the identity of the callers.

Stacy (aged 7) said her step dad is 'touching her where she doesn't want'. It happens when her mum is out at work.

Aimee (7) said she was asked to play 'touch, touch' games of 'his privates' and doesn't want to any more. It's someone in her family and she is scared to tell anyone who it is. In the end she decided she will tell her mum.

Ruby (7) said her uncle was putting his hands on her and it was making her feel sad. She wants it to stop but doesn't think she can tell mum.

David (10): 'My dad sometimes takes me out after school. Mum doesn't know but he always comes with another man and they touch me. It hurts, but I can't stop them. Dad said he will kill mum if I tell anyone.'

Tracey (14) said: 'I'm calling about my dad.' There was a long pause, and then she said: 'My dad does things to me. I don't like it. It's been going on for a year when my mum goes out to work. It makes me feel dirty.' She hadn't told anyone at all about it before.

Kelly (15) rang to say that her mum's boyfriend was 'coming on to her'. She said: 'I told my mum, but she said that I was leading him on.' Kelly went on to say that she was really frightened about what would happen when he came home later that night. With Kelly's permission, the counsellor contacted social services on her behalf, and they arranged for her to stay with relatives. ChildLine subsequently heard that social services and the child protection team were undertaking an investigation into Kelly's situation.

Marie (14) had run away from home and called ChildLine about her dad, who had been sexually abusing her since she was 11. Every time it happened he told her 'if you tell anyone I'm going to kill you'. She wanted to tell her mum what was happening but was afraid of what her mum might do. Marie had run away from home several times before, but always went back because: 'I've got no money and I don't know where to go anyway.' Marie agreed that the police could pick her up from the phone box.

Source: NSPCC

About sexual abuse calls to ChildLine

Of the 13,237 children and young people aged 18 years and under who called ChildLine about sexual abuse in 2007/08:

⇨ For 3,249 (33 per cent) the abuse was categorised as sexual touching;

⇨ For 649 (7 per cent) the abuse was categorised as sexual harassment;

⇨ For 522 (5 per cent) the abuse was categorised as indecency;

⇨ For 156 (2 per cent) the abuse was categorised as organised abuse;

⇨ For 5925 (60 per cent) the abuse was categorised as rape;

⇨ For 244 (2.5 per cent) the abuse was categorised as incest;

⇨ For 3,442 (26 per cent) of calls no specific data was available.

Please note that some children counselled were recorded under more than one category.

About sexual abuse

Sexual abuse occurs when a child or young person is forced or enticed to take part in sexual activities by an adult or other young person. Abuse takes place, whether or not the child is aware of what is happening.

31,392 individuals are currently registered as sex offenders (against both children and adults) in England and Wales (http://press.homeoffice. gov.uk/press-releases/public-protection-working?version=1).
9 February 2009

⇨ The above information is reprinted with kind permission from the NSPCC. Visit www.nspcc.org.uk for more information.

© NSPCC

Behind every statistic, a young victim

UK national centre for tackling the sexual abuse of children announces record third-year results

346 children have been safeguarded in the last three years, the UK's national centre for tackling the sexual abuse of children – the Child Exploitation and Online Protection (CEOP) Centre – announced today.

139 were safeguarded in the last 12 months while over 700 suspected offenders have been arrested since the organisation was launched in April 2006. 334 suspected offenders were arrested in the last year alone.

The figures – published in the organisation's Annual Review for 2008/09 and covering work specifically involving CEOP teams – shows a year-on-year increase as more young children are safeguarded from circumstances of horrific abuse.

As the organisation focuses on the UK's most high-risk child sexual offenders, the CEOP response – in association with local and international forces – has also dismantled or disrupted 166 offender networks since 2006, 82 in the last year.

CEOP also reports that over 4,000,000 UK school children have now seen its unique Thinkuknow education programme about online safety since its launch in 2006, with bespoke resources available for children aged five to 16 years.

Figures, however, only tell part of the story. As the battle against child sex offenders continues apace, the tactics being deployed by those who target children are also evolving.

From studying 5,686 reports received in the last 12 months from the public, industry, charities and other parts of the police, as well as feedback from its education programme, offender interviews and other sources of intelligence, the CEOP Centre reveals the increasing degree to which technology is being used by offenders to target young victims and mask behaviour.

In 2008, CEOP reported that the most significant trend affecting child sexual abuse online was that of convergence such as social networking sites with instant messaging and photo and video sharing.

Now, in 2009, hardware is following the same route, with people increasingly accessing the Internet from a range of devices including computers, games consoles and phones, which provide a much greater freedom of access and movement and often include integrated technology such as cameras. As a result, Internet access is possible from wherever the user may be, placing new and additional responsibilities on parents.

That means that more and more children need to be directly educated on necessary safety measures. CEOP continues to reach out to parents, teachers and other practitioners to help them better understand the threats and adopt the necessary safety steps.

Similarly, CEOP is developing strategies to target offenders who are increasingly trying to use technology to hide their activities such as 'piggybacking' unsecured wireless accounts and hacking.

CEOP also reports that:

⇨ of the 5,686 reports received during the past 12 months – nearly 50% of them from children and adults reporting on behalf of a child – on average four a day still require immediate action as a result of a child being at risk;

⇨ grooming is still the number one offence reported to CEOP, although whereas before this was done primarily via instant messaging, a fast-growing trend is exploiting children through vast, integrated social networking sites;

⇨ offenders are increasingly looking to travel to avoid detection – 73% of missing and high-risk offenders referred to the CEOP Centre during the past year had either travelled or were located overseas;

⇨ and offenders are increasingly using peer-to-peer networks and newsgroups rather than commercial pay-per-view sites in order to share images of sexual abuse.

Jim Gamble is Chief Executive of the CEOP Centre and leads on child protection for the Association of Chief Police Officers (ACPO):

'It is easy to be alarmist about this area of criminality and to suggest that technology is opening doors for offenders to abuse children quicker than we can close them. Well today we put a clear marker down for all to read. If you are a parent, child, social worker, teacher, police officer or indeed an offender, then think of this: every fact and figure we publish today is not just a credit to the CEOP teams but are the results of multi-agency, cross-sector collaboration that is proactively closing those opportunities once and for all.

'Over 4,000,000 UK school children have now been empowered to watch for the dangers and to report them if they feel worried or under threat. More than 25,000 volunteers from teachers to police officers have worked with us and continue to do so in building that programme, to reach not only more children but also to refresh our lesson plans and to go back with new contemporary advice.

Child protection is everybody's business and we should afford our children the same protection online that we would give them in the park or playground

---

'Almost 8,000 professionals have walked through our doors since we opened to receive specialist training and in every force we now have specialist points of contact to share intelligence, identify targets and take action. Not only that but over 50 other organisations from major corporations to specialist service providers have come forward to creatively work with us in making a difference.

'And increasingly our work in areas such as South East Asia and with colleagues in Europe, Australia, Canada and the US is not only shrinking the world for the offender to operate in but is developing and delivering imaginative solutions that are all about inclusion and cross-border application.

'This is not about technology – this is about people. There is no distinction between the online and offline worlds. This is about the behaviour of offenders manipulating any environment to abuse children. Child protection is everybody's business and we should afford our children the same protection online that we would give them in the park or playground – that is our approach and that collective response has already hit home for over 700 suspected offenders and safeguarded almost 350 children.'

The CEOP Centre is the UK's national centre for tackling the abuse of children. A copy of its full Annual Review can be found at ceop.gov.uk/publications. Parents can register for up-to-date safety advice via the site.

⇨ The above information is reprinted with kind permission from the Child Exploitation and Online Protection (CEOP) Centre. Visit www.ceop.police.uk for more information.

© CEOP

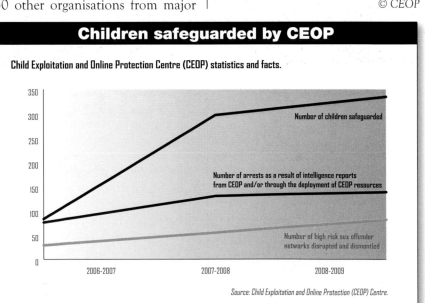

Children safeguarded by CEOP

Child Exploitation and Online Protection Centre (CEOP) statistics and facts.

Number of children safeguarded

Number of arrests as a result of intelligence reports from CEOP and/or through the deployment of CEOP resources

Number of high risk sex offender networks disrupted and dismantled

350 300 250 200 150 100 50 0

2006-2007   2007-2008   2008-2009

Source: Child Exploitation and Online Protection (CEOP) Centre.

Global decrease in child sexual abuse websites

Information from the Internet Watch Foundation

The Internet Watch Foundation (IWF) has published its Annual Report 2008 revealing a fall of nearly 10% in the number of international websites with child sexual abuse content. The report warns against complacency, pointing to the serious nature of the images which are often carried on commercial websites.

The report also highlights the fact that 74% of child sexual abuse domains traced by IWF are commercial operations selling indecent images of children, and 75% of these (some 850 unique domains) are registered with just ten domain name registries. This underlines the importance of recent international efforts with domain name registries to get the site names delisted, and will remain a focus of IWF attention going forward.

'These websites, although reducing in number, represent an extremely serious problem,' said IWF Chief Executive, Peter Robbins OBE, QPM. 'The extensive intelligence networks we have with partner Hotlines and law enforcement colleagues around the world to support international action are making a real difference but the sophisticated way these websites operate still makes it a highly complex and global challenge.'

IWF is the UK self-regulatory body, funded by the Internet industry and the EU, operating a national hotline for public reports of criminal Internet content (www.iwf.org.uk) and providing a notice and take-down service to companies offering web hosting services in the UK. Since 1996 it has dealt with more than 200,000 reports and has over 12 years' experience of tracking and understanding the technologies and behaviour behind the sites. Its 2008 data reveals a continuing trend in the severity and commercialisation of the images:

⇨ 58% of child sexual abuse domains traced contain graphic images involving penetration or torture (47% of domains in 2007);
⇨ 69% of the children appear to be ten years old or younger; 24% six or under, and 4% two or under (80% appeared to be 10 or under in 2007);
⇨ 74% of child sexual abuse domains traced are commercial operations, selling images (80% commercial in 2007);
⇨ It is still rare to trace child sexual abuse content to hosts in the UK (under 1%).

The UK's partnership approach to eradicating child sexual abuse websites is extremely effective, with content being removed within hours by the UK Internet industry.

Lord Stephen Carter CBE, Minister for Communications, Technology and Broadcasting, welcomed the report, 'I have followed the IWF's work for many years and continue to be impressed by the breadth of its industry support and by the range of UK industry-led tactics to combat child sexual abuse content online which have impacted so positively around the world. Effective, widely supported self-regulation is not a simple formula. For the IWF it requires commitment to a range of stakeholder demands, public interest concerns, international political pressures, and technological evolution and I congratulate them on their achievements.'

The greatest challenge remains the global nature of the online distribution of child sexual abuse images. The IWF is convinced that only concerted international law enforcement action, in partnership with hotlines, can tackle the remaining core of sites.

The greatest challenge remains the global nature of the online distribution of child sexual abuse images

---

The IWF suggests five ways to tackle this global problem:

1. Public/private partnership involving service providers working through a system of self-regulation.
2. National notice and take-down schemes to remove criminal online content quickly.
3. Promotion of filtering services to prevent accidental access to websites containing child sexual abuse content.
4. Partnership with domain name registries to delist domain names that sell child sexual abuse images.
5. Sharing data, intelligence and tactics internationally to combat the cross-border nature of these crimes.

29 April 2009

⇨ The above information is reprinted with kind permission from the Internet Watch Foundation. Visit www.iwf.org.uk for more information.

© Internet Watch Foundation

Social networking

Information from ThinkuKnow

There are a number of things to think about when using social networking sites:

Be careful what information you give out...

Be careful what information you give out on your profile. Remember that you don't know who your friends' friends are... or your friends' friends' friends! And you don't know what they'll do with your picture or your phone number if you give it out by mistake. Once your picture is out there, it's out there forever and you won't be able to get it back.

Be aware that information on your profile could potentially be viewed by anyone

Be aware that information on your profile could potentially be viewed by anyone. So if you wouldn't be comfortable printing it off and handing it out on the street, maybe it shouldn't be on your profile. Use a nickname or your initials instead of your name – you don't want just anyone knowing who you are. Consider changing your photo to a cool graphic or picture of your favourite band, that way strangers won't have access to a picture of you.

Think through who you want to chat to...

Think through who you want to chat to, and how many of your personal thoughts you want anyone to view. Sometimes, it can seem a good idea to share what you got up to with your boyfriend last night, or the argument you had with your best mate; but as you're writing – remember that information could be public forever! It is tempting to share loads of stuff on your profile, especially since you're often typing from the comfort of your

own home. But remember, the Internet is a public space. Test yourself by asking 'would I want my teacher/Mum/Dad/ stranger on the train to see this?!' If the answer's no... don't post it!

Be careful who you agree to accept...

Be careful who you agree to accept into your forums/private chat areas. Unfortunately because there are so many young people using these sites, adults with bad intentions will use them to make contact with children too; so you're safer to only chat to people you know in the real world. If you know someone... who knows someone... who knows someone, it doesn't make them your friend, so think carefully about whether you should be chatting to them and what kind of things you're saying.

Know where to go for help...

If you feel anyone is being weird with you or your friends, or if someone is bullying you on one of these sites, contact the administrator of the chat area. If they don't get back to you, you might want to think twice about using the site again.

If it's really serious – like you think the person contacting you may be an adult who wants to abuse you or your mates – report the issue on this thinkuknow site using the red reporting button.

Things to think through

⇨ Use your Privacy Settings! Adjust your account settings (sometimes called 'Privacy Settings') so only approved friends can instant

message you. This won't ruin your social life – new people can still send you friend requests and message you, they just won't be able to pester you via IM. This means that people you don't want to see your profile can't!

⇨ Some social networking sites are really well run and the administrators will try to help you remember to keep your personal information to yourself. Others are not so good – so be careful when choosing which areas you go to.

⇨ Only upload pictures that you'd be happy for your mum to see – anything too sexy to be passed round the dinner table should NOT make it onto the web, as you don't know who could be looking at it or what they might be doing with it.

⇨ Don't post your phone number or email address on your homepage. Think about it – why would anyone actually need this info when they can message you privately via your social networking site?

⇨ Don't post pictures of you or your mates wearing school uniform – if dodgy people see your school badge, they can work out where you are and find you. The more anonymous you are, the less vulnerable you are to people with bad intentions.

⇨ Tick the 'no pic forwarding' option on your MySpace settings page – this will stop people forwarding your pictures to anyone without your consent.

⇨ Don't give too much away in a blog. Yes, tell the world you're going to a party on Saturday night. But don't post details of where it is. Real friends can phone you to get details, why would a complete stranger need to know this information?

⇨ The above information is re-printed with kind permission from ThinkuKnow. Visit www.thinkuknow. co.uk for more information.

© CEOP

'Sexting' amongst UK teens

Leading children's charity Beatbullying uncovers true extent of 'sexting' amongst UK teens

Leading UK children's charity, Beatbullying, today unveils new research on 'sexting', the sending of sexually explicit messages via text and email. The research indicates that over a third (38%) of under-18s have received an offensive or distressing sexual image via text or email.

These findings form part of groundbreaking research on sexting from Beatbullying, the UK's leading bullying prevention charity.

Beatbullying findings uncovers that sexualised peer-to-peer anti social behaviour is escalating at an alarming rate with developments in digital technology.

Common 'sexts' include images of young boys exposing themselves or masturbating, boys who have requested girls to remove their clothing and images of sexual acts which would be considered by most as pornographic.

Material is often Bluetoothed, added to home-built websites, uploaded onto social networking groups and sent around by email or text.

⇨ 38% said they had received a sexually explicit or distressing text or email (male: 36%, female: 39%);

⇨ 70% of young people knew the sender of the message;

⇨ 45% of messages were from a peer, 23% from a current boyfriend/girlfriend and just 2% from adults;

⇨ Of the 25% who received an offensive sexual image, 55% were issued via mobile phone;

⇨ 29% have been chatting online chat when someone started talking about offensive or upsetting sexual things (male: 24%, female: 31%);

⇨ In this instance, 45% said the chat was instigated by a peer, 10% by an ex-partner and 2% by an adult.

These statistics support Beatbullying's work by providing further evidence to highlight that peer-to-peer anti-social/predatory behaviour is one of the biggest threats facing our young people today online and via mobile phones.

Emma-Jane Cross, chief executive of Beatbullying, said: 'Beatbullying surveyed 2,000 young people to understand how technology is changing the way they're communicating and look at how they're manipulating digital media to bully and pressurise their peers.

'We don't want to inhibit young people in their exploration of sexuality, but it is important that parents and schools are aware that sexting is a significant issue amongst our children and young people, so together we can act to stop this kind of behaviour before it escalates into something far more problematic. This is about campaigning for the rights of our young people and for digital safety. We need to address the fact that sexual peer-to-peer contact is being exponentially facilitated through new technologies.

'The Byron report made a commitment to protecting our young people in this complicated new online era, the Government has a duty to ensure it meets these recommendations.

'We need to take serious note of what has happened in the US and Australia. To avoid similar cases here, politicians must work together with organisations like Beatbullying to create an intervention and prevention task force in schools and communities.

'This needs to be part of the solution if we are to educate our young people, teachers and families about the consequences of their actions and how to keep safe online as well as offline.'

In a major step to tackle the bullying epidemic head on, Beatbullying launched the world's first peer mentoring social networking site www.cybermentors.org.uk in March 2009. For the first time, a young person suffering at the hands of bullies both on and offline can seek immediate help and support from their peers.

Since its launch in March, over 150,000 young people have accessed Beatbullying's CyberMentors website to seek help and support from their peers.

Definition of sexting

A portmanteau of sex and texting, sexting is the act of sending sexually explicit messages or photos electronically, primarily between mobile phones and/or the Internet. Sexting is an extension of cyberbullying when someone (or a group of people) deliberately attempts to hurt, upset, threaten or humiliate someone else. This includes when a recipient is made to feel uncomfortable as a direct result of the content, or asked to do something which makes the recipient feel distressed.

4 August 2009

⇨ The above information is reprinted with kind permission from Beatbullying. Visit www.beatbullying.org for more information.

© Beatbullying

Teen domestic violence statistics

Information from Women's Aid

National domestic violence charity Women's Aid has launched new teenage domestic violence statistics with *Bliss* magazine as part of their Expect Respect campaign. The statistics, which launch in the January edition of the magazine, show that approximately one in five *Bliss* readers have been physically hurt by someone they were dating – and for 16-year-old girls, this goes up to one in four. The survey, which was live on the *Bliss* magazine website in September, also showed that nearly a quarter of 14-year-old girls have been forced to have sex or do something else sexual they didn't want to do by someone they were dating.

Women's Aid Chief Executive, Nicola Harwin CBE said:

'Although we know that one in four women experience domestic violence, it is still shocking to find out that this statistic applies equally to teenage girls in their very first relationships. It is also worrying that our survey showed that, the older girls are, the more likely they are to accept being bullied and controlled, whereas they are less likely to confide in parents and ask for help. Whether it is physical violence, forced sex, or emotional abuse, this abuse is never justified. Women's Aid is working to prevent abuse in the future by working with *Bliss* magazine to publicise our new resources for young people, parents and teachers, and to send out the message that we should all Expect Respect in our relationships.'

Leslie Sinoway, Editor of *Bliss*, said:

'*Bliss* magazine and mybliss.co.uk are delighted to be in partnership with Women's Aid for the excellent Expect Respect campaign. As a brand, *Bliss* has always been committed to equipping teen girls with the skills, knowledge and confidence they need to ensure that they go on to have happy, healthy relationships. We hope this campaign will help educate young girls in what is, and what is not, acceptable behaviour from a partner.'

The Expect Respect campaign has been running since September when it launched on The Hideout website for young people affected by domestic violence, supported by *Hollyoaks* actors Ashley Slanina-Davies and Kieron Richardson, who play Amy and Ste in the Channel 4 programme. The campaign asks young people to both Expect Respect and give respect in their relationships and aims to work with teenagers now to reduce the amount of domestic violence experienced in the future.

Ashley Slanina-Davies said: 'Domestic abuse takes many forms, it can be physical, sexual or mental. In *Hollyoaks*, my character Amy faced this in her relationship with Ste and I know from this storyline why it can be difficult to leave an abusive relationship. If domestic violence is affecting your life in any way, you can go to www.thehideout.org.uk for support and information. The important thing to remember is that there is always someone willing to listen so don't suffer in silence.'

Kieron Richardson said: 'Domestic violence affects many young people, whether in their relationships with each other or if they have grown up with violence in their homes. From playing Ste on *Hollyoaks* I can imagine how frightening it would be to have him as a boyfriend. Violence and bullying in relationships is always unacceptable. Everyone should Expect Respect in all of their relationships, and not only expect to be respected but to give respect to others as well.'

Young people affected by domestic violence or who are interested in the Expect Respect campaign can go to the redeveloped Hideout website www.thehideout.org.uk, which now contains a range of new interactive features with separate areas for children and teenagers and includes an online messageboard for young people.

3 December 2008

⇨ The above information is reprinted with kind permission from Women's Aid. Visit www.womensaid.org.uk for more information on this and other related topics.

© *Women's Aid Federation of England*

Protecting children from sexual abuse

Information from the Home Office

At least ten children have been protected from potential abuse by sex offenders in the first six months of the government's child sexual offender disclosure pilot.

This early success has led to the decision to extend the scheme within the police forces involved. From today, the pilot will be extended force-wide in Cleveland, Cambridgeshire and Hampshire (including the Isle of Wight). The fourth pilot site, Warwickshire, is already force-wide.

Pilot's progress – six months on

Since the pilot launched six months ago, provisional management information which has been provided by the police forces shows there have been a total of 153 enquiries and 79 applications from parents, carers and guardians. Ten disclosures have taken place.

> **There have been a total of 153 enquiries and 79 applications from parents, carers and guardians. Ten disclosures have taken place**

Under the terms of the pilot, launched in September 2008, a parent, carer or guardian can request that an individual who has access to their child or children is checked out for a record of child sexual offences.

If this individual is found to have convictions for sexual offences against children, and poses a risk of causing serious harm to the child or children concerned, then this information may be disclosed to the person best placed to protect the child – usually the parent, carer or guardian.

Statement from the Home Secretary

Jacqui Smith said, 'Protecting children and families from sex offenders is one of my top priorities and the UK has one of the most robust systems of managing sex offenders in the world. Today's results are extremely encouraging – this pilot has provided crucial protection for children who might otherwise be at risk.

'The development of this scheme – in consultation with Sara Payne, the police and children's charities – has been a major step forward in our ability to protect children from sex offenders but also to empower parents and guardians to understand how to best protect their children.

'There will be a full evaluation of the pilot at the end of the year and if it concludes that the pilot has been a success then I will be seeking to roll out the scheme nationally.'

Under the terms of the pilot, both the child and the subject must live within the pilot site area, which means that there is the potential to protect even more children in these areas.

Statement from Association of Chief Police Officers (ACPO)

Keith Bristow, Chief Constable of Warwickshire Police and ACPO lead on violence and public protection, said, 'Today's announcement by the Home Secretary to extend the child sex offender disclosure pilot across its four sites gives us an opportunity to increase our understanding of how we share information to keep children and young people safe from harm. Britain has one of the most effective and respected systems for managing child sex offenders in the world. Managed disclosure where parents, carers and guardians have concerns about a named individual in contact with children is part of that process.

'To date, three of the four forces (Cambridgeshire, Cleveland and Hampshire) have been operating the pilot across parts of the force, with Warwickshire operating it force-wide. Extending the pilot sites across the forces will allow better evaluation on which to base future decisions. Information from the pilot so far, with over 150 enquiries, has led to ten disclosures being made.

'The police service is committed to protecting children from any individual who poses harm or risk and the pilot has assisted in raising public awareness of child protection issues. For those parents and carers who have made enquiries, we trust that it has helped give them confidence that their children are safe.'

Statement from Victims' Champion, Sara Payne

Sara Payne, Victims' Champion, said: 'This is great news for the disclosure pilot schemes in Cleveland, Cambridge and Hampshire (Warwickshire have been county wide from the start in September of 2008). This shows that they are working well and the police are pleased with the outcomes thus far. It was entirely right for them to start in smaller areas and to get used to all things new but as they have found this will prove to be an invaluable tool to both police and carers alike. I am as always keeping a close eye on the progression of the pilots and will have the real results of the evaluation by the end of the year.'
16 March 2009

⇨ The above information is reprinted with kind permission from the Home Office. Visit www.homeoffice.gov.uk for more information.

© Crown copyright

The dangers of Sarah's law

There may be many as 250,000 people in Britain with an active sexual interest in children when only 30,000 have been caught, convicted and registered

By Jeremy Sare

New Statesman readers who are also habitual viewers of *Eastenders* may constitute a fairly small demographic. But you may at least be aware of the current furore over the soap's portrayal of a father's sexual abuse of his 15-year-old stepdaughter.

The vast majority of child abusers have no convictions

There may be some justification for the hundreds complaining about these distressing issues being presented in prime time: equally it is courageous for the Beeb to include a scenario which challenges the public's perception of what is a 'typical paedophile'.

The repellent Tony's grooming and seduction of his stepdaughter, Whitney, is a much more familiar pattern of abuse than the more commonly held image of predators lurking in parks. NSPCC say over 75 per cent of offenders are closely known to the victim.

By unhappy coincidence, the Home Office launched last week, with an unashamed tilt at populism, their pilots for 'Sarah's Law'. Under the scheme, worried parents can be told details about anyone with direct access to their child, who has a conviction for a sexual offence.

Community disclosure, the brainchild of former Home Secretary John Reid, is aimed specifically at single mothers who are often entrapped into relationships by paedophiles targeting the children.

However, the abusive stepfather in *Eastenders* has no convictions for sexual crimes. If Whitney's mum, Bianca, asked for a check under Sarah's Law, her Tony would get the all-clear. The NSPCC, who are advising the BBC scriptwriters, reject the government's claim the new procedure is certain to enhance child protection. Head of Policy, Diane Sutton feared Sarah's Law's ability to 'create a false sense of security'.

The vast majority of child abusers have no convictions at all. Criminologist Mark Williams-Thomas estimates there may be as many as 250,000 people in Britain with an active sexual interest in children when only 30,000 have been caught, convicted and signed the sex offender's register. The trouble with Sarah's Law, is it hardens the public's view that the threat to children's safety comes predominantly from convicted paedophiles. The new parental right for information on offenders is, in effect, an illusion of empowerment.

The Home Office consulted on Sarah's Law with a host of children's charities as well as police and probation services. Their almost universal opposition proved no brake to ministers who preferred to listen to the views of victims' groups than the recognised experts in offender management. One officer from the Met put it harshly when he said, 'just because you've been in a car crash doesn't make you an accident investigator'.

The minister responsible for child protection, Vernon Coaker, insists police will only divulge such information which is, 'relevant, necessary and proportionate'. Parents are to be warned they face prosecution if they share the information with others. But there is no real prospect of this experiment remaining 'in vitro' when the stakes are as high as the protection of children. People talk. Parents are not so selfish to be solely concerned about their own child's safety and not their friend's and neighbour's. Some would see a fine for a breach of a 'paedo's' confidentiality a price worth paying or even a badge of honour.

The Home Office has also turned a blind eye to the thoroughly negative experience of the US on widening disclosure. Under Megan's Law, known as community notification, there is unfettered access to databases containing details on thousands of offenders including their addresses and photographs.

Reports of low-level violence aimed at registered sex offenders is fairly common but public disorder

and outright vigilantism less so. One notorious case was William Elliott from Maine who had a conviction for 'sex abuse with a minor'. His offence was to sleep with his 15-year-old sweetheart, three months before her 16th birthday. Years later, loner Stephen Marshall looked William up on Maine's sex offender website, located his trailer home and shot him dead with a .45 Magnum.

> ## The lessons from the US are clear; widespread community knowledge of offenders leads directly to their hounding and isolation

Scott Taylor is Chief of Community Corrections in Oregon and has worked with sex offenders for over 30 years. When asked what would be the ideal system for managing them he described, 'a multi-agency approach where police, probation and prison officials would meet regularly to assess risk and determine appropriate monitoring levels of all offenders. If we had that we probably wouldn't need community notification [Megan's Law].' The picture he painted was an uncannily close portrayal of the UK's Multi-Agency Public Protection Arrangements (MAPPA).

In many states, Megan's Law has been compromised by locally elected officials imposing undeniably tough but ultimately pointless conditions on offenders. Compelling them to be identified on their driving licences, by banners on their front doors or even on their car number plates only adds to their further vilification. It is not surprising to hear the outcome, in many areas, is a third of registered offenders disappearing from the authorities. Even if they stay in touch, many refuse to provide a home address. Detective Bob Schilling of Seattle Police Department conceded, '50 per cent of the city's highest risk offenders declare themselves homeless'.

The lessons from the US are clear; widespread community knowledge of offenders leads directly to their hounding and isolation. Ultimately the policy is self-defeating; an offender who has gone to ground is an unmanaged offender and a greater risk to children. Martin Narey, CEO of Barnardo's echoed this fear last week when he spoke of his 'grave concerns' and added bluntly, 'Sarah's Law will put children in greater danger'. Other measures, such as last week's proposal to compel released offenders to undergo polygraph testing as part of their probation, has a much stronger evidence base from the US in reducing harm to children.

Dan Norris, Labour MP for Wansdyke, is a strong supporter of the government's disclosure pilots but he also stresses the need for substantial public education. 'Information on offenders alone doesn't protect children. I have seen in the US how it needs to be combined with a community education programme. If we don't do the same we'll be missing a trick. Educated parents are able to make properly informed dispassionate decisions.'

But, in the context of child protection, it is always going to be hard to disentangle the rational from the raw emotion. Child abuse immediately makes parents raise a psychological drawbridge and are then oblivious to where dangers to their children really lie. John Reid himself struggled to hide his personal feelings. Although he claimed the cause was driven by a simple conviction,

'such information [on sex offenders] should not be the sole preserve of officialdom', last June's Child Sex Offenders Review was announced with the grisly promise of instigating chemical castration.

Reid's successor, Jacqui Smith, in place of justification just offers us ethereal banalities such as, 'I want to see every child living their lives free from fear.' Well, who doesn't? A home secretary should be providing the public with practical solutions rather than floating some utopian aspiration.

The producers of *Eastenders*, labouring under a welter of tabloid protest and viewers' complaints, are attempting to make people get past the initial revulsion of the act of abuse and accept the grim fact that 'paedophiles' are very often members of the same family. A BBC spokeswoman said, 'we appreciate that for some viewers this storyline will have particular resonance and significance. In running it, it's certainly not our intention to cause distress or upset, either to those who've suffered from sexual abuse or their families. Our aim is instead to raise awareness of this very sensitive issue.'

The producers' dilemma is instructive to children's charities and ministers alike on how to confront the issue in a digestible manner which can stimulate an objective debate. If it does, it won't be thanks to Sarah's Law.

22 September 2008

© *New Statesman*

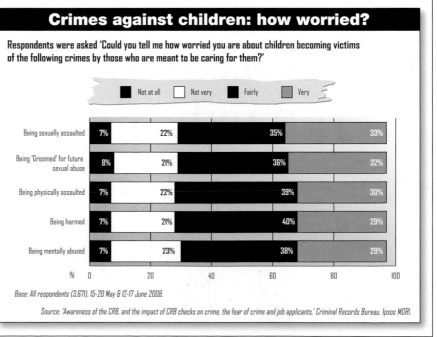

Crimes against children: how worried?

Respondents were asked 'Could you tell me how worried you are about children becoming victims of the following crimes by those who are meant to be caring for them?'

Legend: Not at all | Not very | Fairly | Very

	Not at all	Not very	Fairly	Very
Being sexually assaulted	7%	22%	35%	33%
Being 'Groomed' for future sexual abuse	8%	21%	36%	32%
Being physically assaulted	7%	22%	39%	30%
Being harmed	7%	21%	40%	29%
Being mentally abused	7%	23%	38%	29%

Base: All respondents (3,671). 15-20 May & 12-17 June 2008.

Source: 'Awareness of the CRB, and the impact of CRB checks on crime, the fear of crime and job applicants.' Criminal Records Bureau. Ipsos MORI.

Adult survivors of child abuse

Information from Breathing Space

What is sexual abuse?

Sexual abuse is any sexually related behaviour between two or more people where there is an imbalance of power. This can include adult-child, older child-younger child, adolescent-younger person, or any situation where the other person is forced to participate. It is sexually abusive when the victim is unaware of the abuse (such as being watched while bathing, using the bathroom, changing, etc.), as well as when the victim is sleeping, unconscious, under the influence of alcohol or drugs, or is too young, naïve, or able to understand what is going on.

Remember you are not alone and that you can get help.

How might this affect me?

The impact of sexual abuse can range from no apparent effects to very severe ones. Typically, children who experience the most serious types of abuse – abuse involving family members and high degrees of physical force – exhibit behaviour problems ranging from separation anxiety to post-traumatic stress disorder. However, children who are the victims of sexual abuse are also often exposed to a variety of other stressors and difficult circumstances in their lives, including parental substance abuse. The sexual abuse and its aftermath may be only part of the child's negative experiences and subsequent behaviours. Therefore, correctly diagnosing abuse is often complex. Conclusive physical evidence of sexual abuse is relatively rare in suspected cases. For all of these reasons, when abuse is suspected, an appropriately trained health professional should be consulted.

Effects of abuse

Being abused as a child may have serious and long-lasting effects on a person. Such effects can include:

⇨ Loss of confidence, dignity and self-respect;
⇨ Low self-esteem and poor self-worth;
⇨ Loss of hope for the future;
⇨ Adverse effects on both physical and mental health;
⇨ The inability to trust others even close family and friends;
⇨ The inability to relax and enjoy life;
⇨ Loss of innocence and childhood;
⇨ Anxiety, guilt and fear;
⇨ Sexual dysfunction, withdrawal, and acting out;
⇨ Difficulties in relating to the opposite sex.

And may also lead to:

⇨ Alcohol and drug abuse;
⇨ Obsessive behaviour and strict routines;
⇨ Anxiety states;
⇨ Self-harming, e.g. cutting, scratching or burning;
⇨ Depression and suicide.

Physical effects and behaviour changes in abused children

The most obvious signs of childhood sexual abuse are the physical factors.

⇨ Children that are being sexually abused may have difficulty walking or sitting, have stained, torn or bloody clothing, or have pain or itching in the genital area;
⇨ Some children may have bruises or external bleeding, vaginal bleeding or anal bleeding.

Children may also show certain behaviour characteristics that may point to childhood sexual abuse.

⇨ These include a highly sexual form of play, bizarre or unusual knowledge of sex, and unusually seductive behaviours with peers;
⇨ Children may also have poor relationships with peers, be delinquent, run away, or even threaten or attempt suicide;
⇨ Teachers may also see deterioration in school work or sudden noticeable changes in behaviour;
⇨ The child may become overly concerned about siblings;
⇨ The child may even exhibit fear of physical contact.

Some general facts

⇨ One in four girls and one in six boys are subjected to some form of sexual abuse;
⇨ In more than 75% of cases the

abuse is committed by an adult the child knows and trusts;

⇨ Most abusers are men but women are also capable of sexual abuse;

⇨ Child sexual abuse is any type of sexual assault of a child under 16.

Sexual abuse takes many forms

⇨ Fondling a child's genitals;

⇨ Masturbation;

⇨ Oral-genital contact;

⇨ Digital penetration;

⇨ Vaginal and anal intercourse.

Child sexual abuse is not solely restricted to physical contact; such abuse could include non-contact abuse, such as exposure, voyeurism, and child pornography.

Why do children not speak out?

During the time that the abuse is taking place a child may say nothing. This may be as a result of:

⇨ Threats with further abuse and violence if they tell anyone;

⇨ Fear that they will not be believed;

⇨ Believing it was their fault that the abuse happened;

⇨ An inability to describe or understand what has happened to them;

⇨ Wanting to protect the family or even the abuser(s), who could be either male or female.

Child sexual abuse victims may temporarily block memories of what has happened but the effects will surface as they grow. Not talking about what happened will not make it go away but encourages it to fester. Adults often do not talk about child sexual abuse because of their own discomfort with the topic. If adults are not willing to talk about the abuse, the child will probably feel there is something to be ashamed of, that it is dirty and just too awful to talk about. This attitude will only serve to increase the child's feelings of guilt, shame and feelings of being abnormal and will compound their problems.

Children often feel powerless to stop the abuse. You cannot be responsible for consenting to an act you did not understand or which you were forced into.

Why has this happened to me?

Remember, the abuser is always to blame for the abuse, not the victim.

No matter how long ago you were abused, your feelings about what happened to you are important. You have the right to be listened to, no matter what you want to say. Through speaking about your abuse you may well be able to overcome any difficulties that you experience as an adult.

Who are the perpetrators of child sexual abuse?

The majority of sexual offenders are family members or are otherwise known to the child. Sexual abuse by strangers is not nearly as common as sexual abuse by family members. Men perpetrate most instances of sexual abuse, but there are cases in which women are the offenders. Despite a common myth, homosexual men are not more likely to sexually abuse children than heterosexual men are. *If you live in Scotland and would like to talk to someone about the issues raised in this article, you can call Breathing Space free on 0800 83 85 87. If you are calling from outside Scotland and would like to contact Breathing Space for further advice, you can call this number on a mobile phone to speak to an advisor (network charges may vary).*

⇨ The above information is reprinted with kind permission from Breathing Space. Visit www.breathingspacescotland.co.uk for more information.

© Breathing Space

Abused children 'need therapy'

Information from the Press Association

Thousands of sexually abused children could suffer long-term mental health problems because of a massive shortfall in the availability of therapy, the NSPCC has said.

Every year up to 88,500 sex abuse victims across the UK are left struggling to recover from their ordeal because of a 'postcode lottery' in provision of therapeutic services, the children's charity warned.

A new report found there was less than one support programme per 10,000 children in England, Northern Ireland and Scotland – figures for Wales were not available – with some areas apparently offering nothing at all.

Even when therapy was available it was an average of three months before the young victims saw a professional, and in some cases they had to wait a year.

Some therapeutic services are so over-stretched they are closing their waiting lists altogether, researchers said.

Teenagers were found to be particularly likely to miss out on therapy because they may be considered too old for support on a child protection plan but are less able to access services for adults.

The NSPCC's Debbie Allnock, who led the research, said the severe shortage of therapeutic services was a serious problem that needed 'huge' investment.

'Sexual abuse can have devastating consequences for a child but it remains a low priority within mainstream mental health services and among local authorities,' she said.

'Yet experiences of sexual abuse are common among people with severe long-term behavioural, criminal and addiction problems.'

'Long waiting lists mean that if a young person is sexually abused they often don't get the therapeutic help they need unless they also have a child protection plan.'
19 July 2009

⇨ The above information is reprinted with kind permission from the Press Association. Visit www.pressassociation.com for more information.

© The Press Association

The nightmare of false memories of sexual abuse

Despite the falling away of media interest, families are still being torn apart when 'recovered' memories of childhood sexual abuse are introduced into the minds of vulnerable people

By Chris French, editor of *Skeptic* magazine

I have three wonderful daughters – two teenagers and one young adult. I can hardly imagine anything more horrible than the prospect that one of them might one day enter therapy for help with some common psychological problem such as anxiety, insomnia or depression and, at the end of that process, accuse me of childhood sexual abuse on the basis of 'recovered' memories. Even though I would know with absolute certainty that such allegations were untrue, the chances are that nothing I could say or do would convince my accusers of this.

A few days ago I sat in a lecture theatre mostly filled with middle-aged or elderly parents living through this exact nightmare. Typically, their adult children had started therapy with no pre-existing memories of being sexually abused, but had become convinced during the therapeutic process that they had indeed been victimised in this way. So convinced were they that the 'recovered' memories were true, they more often than not accused their parents directly of this vile act and then cut off any further contact, leaving their parents devastated and confused, their lives shattered.

The occasion in question was the 15th Annual General Meeting of the British False Memory Society. The BFMS began life in 1993, the year after the formation of the False Memory Syndrome Foundation in the US. Accused parents were at the forefront of founding both organisations. Both have scientific and professional advisory boards to support them in their aims, which include providing support – including legal assistance where necessary – to those affected by such accusations, providing information and advice to professionals, and improving our understanding of false memories by encouraging and supporting academic and professional research.

One serious problem appears to be that many people mistakenly believe that the false memory controversy is 'yesterday's news'. They are aware that there was a huge increase in such allegations back in the 1980s and 1990s. They may even be aware that many professionals and academics have reacted against such claims, most notably Elizabeth Loftus, whose pioneering work in this area has done more to increase our understanding of the true nature of false memories than any other scientist. But it is simply not the case that this is a dead issue.

Although the incidence of new cases is much reduced from when the controversy was at its peak, new cases do still come to light with depressing frequency, as the files of the BFMS can attest. Furthermore, the fallout from the peak period is still very much with us. There are still many families throughout the world being torn apart by these accusations, many of whom will sadly never achieve any kind of reconciliation.

One intriguing aspect of this awful situation is why the media generally appeared to lose interest. The press and broadcasters are often guilty of focusing on the human interest angle of stories at the expense of good solid scientific evidence, the MMR controversy being a case in point. As most scientists know, there never really was a 'controversy' over MMR, with the consensus among medical experts being that there is no link between MMR vaccination and autism. But the human interest value of tearful interviews with sobbing mothers supported by the views of a few maverick scientists was always going to be enough to bias the media coverage of this issue, with tragic consequences.

In the case of the false memory controversy, however, there was human interest on both sides of the story. Obviously, sensationalist accounts of 'recovered' memories of brutal childhood sexual abuse – or even better, ritualised Satanic abuse leading to the development of 'multiple personalities' – were always going to be tempting to a certain type of journalist, despite the lack of any good scientific evidence supporting such claims. But we also had the other victims to consider: the accused family members and those around them. Why were their stories given so little coverage?

I got some answers at the BFMS meeting. There are some cases where the accused are willing to go public but are prevented from doing so by legal gagging orders and are thus not free to present their side of the story. But much more common is the situation where the accused do not want to jeopardise their chances of obtaining the one thing they want more than anything else in the world: reconciliation with their estranged children. Furthermore, to go public with such stories inevitably will invite suspicion. Unless one is very familiar with the scientific research relating to false memories, there may well be the temptation to assume that there's no smoke without fire.

There is a general perception that the public mood is much more volatile with respect to the issue of paedophilia than it used to be. Remember the attack on a paediatrician in Portsmouth by an illiterate mob who did not know the difference between a paediatrician and a paedophile? The episode has often been cited as a prime example of the dangers of adopting a vigilante mentality. The fact that the story appears to be an urban myth is often missed by journalists, who refer to it in sensationalist stories published in the very newspapers that attempted to whip up such sentiments in the first place.

According to an article by Brendan O'Neill on the BBC news website, the incident that gave rise to these stories involved a female paediatrician consultant, Dr Yvette Cloete, in Newport, Gwent (not Portsmouth),

who returned from work to find 'paedo' sprayed on her door, probably by local youngsters. Distressing as this incident was for Dr Cloete, it is a long way from an excited mob threatening physical violence. But for all that, the perception that there may be a violent backlash against anyone even suspected of paedophilia is a strong factor in explaining the reluctance of many accused to go public.

The evidence strongly suggests that far from being unable to remember sexual abuse, victims typically find it all too difficult to keep such memories out of their consciousness

---

There are now many cases of 'retractors' whose stories could potentially be featured in media coverage. Retractors are individuals who initially believed that their memories of abuse were real but later came to realise they were not. Again, one cannot overstate the courage of such individuals in acknowledging that they have put other family members through unimaginable pain and suffering on the basis of a sincerely held but mistaken belief. Understandably, however, such individuals are often too upset and possibly ashamed to want to tell their stories publicly.

It is hard to find a silver lining inside such a grim and depressing cloud, but there is one. Although it may be of little consolation to those who continue to suffer as a consequence of 'recovered' memories, the controversy did trigger a huge amount of research into false memories. Since the mid-1990s, hundreds of papers have been published on the topic and it is probably fair to say that the results have come as something of a surprise even to the researchers themselves. Numerous experiments have shown that it is much easier than anyone might have supposed to implant false

memories in a large minority of the population.

Reliable experimental procedures have been developed to study susceptibility to false memories and we now understand a great deal about the conditions that are most likely to give rise to false memories (for an excellent introduction to the field, read Richard J. McNally's *Remembering Trauma*). It turns out that the conditions typically found in the psychotherapeutic context fit the bill perfectly. Specifically, a vulnerable individual being informed by the therapist, an authority figure, that their current psychological symptoms strongly indicate that they must have been abused as children even if they can no longer remember the abuse due to repression. Once this has been accepted by the client, they are encouraged to engage in a range of mental exercises to 'recover' these memories, but which in fact are highly likely to result in the formation of false memories.

It is not surprising that many people find it easy to believe that when apparent memories of childhood abuse are reported for the first time during psychotherapy, they probably are based upon events which did take place. After all, we know that such abuse really does take place with alarming frequency and can sometimes have devastating effects upon the victims. We're also all familiar with the Freudian notion of repression – the idea that when something happens that is so awful, the mind will automatically bury it as a defence mechanism so that one could not remember it consciously no matter how hard one tried. This idea has been at the centre of countless novels and movies, which often portray the heroic struggle of the victim and therapist to dig deep into the unconscious mind to retrieve those corrosive memories so that healing can begin.

The problem is that there is very little evidence to support the existence of repression as conceptualised by Freud. The evidence strongly suggests that far from being unable to remember sexual abuse, victims typically find it all too difficult to keep such memories out of their consciousness.

My own interest in this topic was initially triggered by my wish to try to explain reports of anomalous experiences such as alien abduction claims and hypnotic past-life regression. Although many people find it plausible that psychotherapy allows people to retrieve repressed memories of childhood abuse, should it not give us pause for thought that exactly the same 'memory recovery' techniques, including hypnotic regression and guided imagery, can give rise to apparent memories of being taken on board spaceships and medically examined by aliens, or a former incarnation as Napoleon?

The writer and broadcaster Karl Sabbagh addressed the meeting on Saturday and considered an uncomfortable topic that will have occurred to any intelligent person reflecting upon the work of organisations like the BFMS and its American counterpart. Even if most of the parents attending the meeting were in fact innocent victims of false memory, isn't it possible that at least some are perpetrators of abuse hiding behind the scientific evidence for false memories? I had, of course, reflected at length on this issue myself and it has to be acknowledged that it is a possibility.

However, I feel that if I were a perpetrator I may well protest my innocence but I doubt I would join a group that aims to keep this issue in the public eye. I would instead want to sweep it under the carpet and hope that everyone would forget about it. As Sabbagh asks in his new book *Remembering Our Childhood: How Memory Betrays Us*, 'After all, if sex abusers all band together and pretend to be innocent, why aren't there established societies of murderers, burglars, and embezzlers doing the same thing?'

Chris French is a professor of psychology at Goldsmiths, University of London, where he heads the Anomalistic Psychology Research Unit. He is a member of the scientific and professional advisory board of the British False Memory Society, and edits the UK version of Skeptic *magazine.*
8 April 2009
© Guardian News & Media Ltd 2009

New research sparks fear over paedophile convictions

Child safety campaigners fear dangerous paedophiles could escape conviction because of new research by Midland boffins

A study by Warwick University and Leicester University has backed up claims that False Memory Syndrome exists.

The controversial psychological condition, which claims childhood memories are not real, was previously discredited after paedophiles in the US used it to claim sex abuse allegations were made up.

'For these researchers to dismiss people's abuse as being the result of a foggy memory is very insulting'

And Claude Knights, Director of children's charity Kidscape, has warned that the new Midland research could again be hijacked by paedophiles to discredit their victims in court.

She said: 'This debate goes back to the 1990s and the idea of False Memory Syndrome where this kind of research was first misused and has been ever since then.

'Paedophiles live in an alternative moral universe to the rest of us and will use anything they can to justify their perverted image of children.

'Of course there are pros and cons with all scientific research and I would not get in the way of academic progress but we must be careful this research does not get hijacked.'

Sex abuse victim Steve Bevan, of the support group Survivors Swindon, agrees the new research could be dangerous.

He said: 'I understand the need for research in this area but I've read this report and I don't agree with its findings one bit.

'Every person I have ever worked with knows exactly what happened to  them, and how, in every horrible detail.

'So for these researchers to dismiss people's abuse as being the result of a foggy memory is very insulting.'

False Memory Syndrome was first identified in the early 1990s in the US as a damaging side effect of a psychological treatment called Recovered Memory Therapy.

This was fashionable in the late 80s and early 90s when therapists related clients' problems to abuse in childhood – usually sexual and often inflicted by the father.

False Memory Syndrome was first identified in the early 1990s in the US as a damaging side effect of a psychological treatment called Recovered Memory Therapy

---

It involved putting the patient under hypnosis or interpreting their dreams to unlock memories which therapists believed were repressed by the conscious mind, often for decades.

But the practice was largely discredited, leading to militant paedophile groups, such as the Paedophile Information Exchange, claiming sex abuse convictions were unsafe.

The first case of False Memory Syndrome in the UK was reported in 1990 and the British False Memory Society was founded three years later. It is now aware of 1,600 families who have been affected by false accusations across Britain.

And Madeline Greenhalgh, director of the British False Memory Society, believes the number who do come forward is just the tip of the iceberg.

She said: 'From our point of view this study is good news and confirms what we have known all along, which is that memories are very unreliable.

'But people must keep this issue in context and realise that judges realise memories are fallible and that this is a matter of common sense for all involved.'

Midland researchers Kimberley Wade and Carla Laney were unavailable for comment.
14 July 2008

⇨ The above information is reprinted with kind permission from the *Sunday Mercury*. Visit www.sundaymercury. net for more information.

© *Sunday Mercury*

EU steps up fight against trafficking and child abuse

New laws to protect the most vulnerable people against terrible crimes

The European Commission is calling for tougher laws against human trafficking and the sexual abuse of children, saying current efforts to combat these crimes don't reflect their scale and gravity.

Globally an estimated 1.2 million people are trafficked every year, mainly for cheap labour and sexual services. Most are women and girls.

There are few reliable statistics on the number of people trafficked into or within Europe, but it is probably of the order of several hundred thousand. Yet in 2006, the most recent year for which numbers are available, prosecutors brought just 1,500 criminal trafficking cases to court. Only 3,000 victims received assistance.

Trafficking in humans is extremely profitable, and most traffickers are professional and organised criminals. Most are based outside the EU but there are now growing networks inside too, especially since the bloc's eastward expansion.

Under the commission's proposed changes, EU countries are encouraged to prosecute EU nationals for crimes committed in other countries and to draw on investigative methods used for other kinds of organised crime, like tapping phones and tracking criminal money movements.

The proposal calls for better legislative tools to punish traffickers and for more protection and assistance for victims. Independent national bodies would be set up to monitor implementation.

The commission has also revised legislation against the sexual abuse and exploitation of children. Here again, reliable estimates are hard to obtain. But studies suggest certain forms of sexual violence against children are on the rise in Europe and that a significant minority of children in Europe, between 10% and 20%, are sexually assaulted during their childhood.

In particular, the proposal seeks to criminalise use of the Internet to prey on children and to step up enforcement of laws against child pornography. In 2008 more than 1,000 commercial and about 500 non-commercial child abuse content websites were found, about 70% in the US.

On behalf of the commission, the EU agency for fundamental rights is developing ways to measure child welfare in Europe, based on factors related to family environment, protection against exploitation and violence, education and civic responsibility.
25 March 2009

⇨ The above information is reprinted with kind permission from the European Commission. Visit ec.europea.eu for more information.

© *European Commission*

Corporal punishment

Information from politics.co.uk

What is corporal punishment?

Corporal punishment refers to the use of physical punishment to correct behaviour. The term derives from the Latin *corpus*, meaning body.

As an officially administered or sanctioned method of enforcing discipline, corporal punishment is in virtually terminal decline. Despite persistent enthusiasm for physical chastisement in significant sections of the population, social scientists are virtually unanimous in arguing that corporal punishment has more negative than positive effects.

Background

The infliction of physical pain as an official means of punishment is as old as human history.

In the UK's schools and prisons, until relatively recently, physical punishment was perceived as part of the educative and disciplinary process, and was often viewed as 'character building'.

Although the various methods of corporal punishment were steadily outlawed throughout the 20th century, it was not until after the 1967 Plowden report, *Children and their Primary Schools*, that the abolition of corporal punishment in state schools was treated as a major issue, and in 1986 it was outlawed altogether.

It was not until 1998 that corporal punishment was outlawed for the few remaining independent schools that retained the practice.

The issue of corporal punishment must now be considered in light of the Human Rights Act 1998 and the European Convention of Human Rights, particularly Article Three on protection against torture, inhuman or degrading treatment or punishment.

The provisions of the Convention of the Rights of the Child 1989 is also important for child punishment, as Article 19 states: 'Parties shall take all appropriate legislative, administrative, social and educational measures to protect the child from all forms of physical or mental violence, injury or abuse, neglect or negligent treatment, maltreatment or exploitation.'

Controversies

Corporal punishment remains legal when used by parents. Since 1860, parents have been permitted to use 'reasonable chastisement' on their children – and this remains the case today, except in Scotland, which has legislated to ban parental corporal punishment.

In 1995, the Committee on the Rights of the Child, after examining the UK's first report under the UN Convention on the Rights of the Child, recommended that corporal punishment in the family should be prohibited, and criticised the existence of the defence of 'reasonable chastisement'.

Following the 1997 case of A v. UK in the European Court of Human Rights, which found that the defence of 'reasonable chastisement' did not provide sufficient protection for the rights of the child, the Government promised a review.

Despite persistent public enthusiasm for corporal punishment, no mainstream political party in the UK appears intent on reversing the trend of the past 50 years.

Statistics

States with full prohibition of corporal punishment in legislation, where it is prohibited in the home, in schools, in alternative care settings, and in the penal system both as a sentence for crime and as a disciplinary measure, are: Austria, Bulgaria, Chile, Croatia, Cyprus, Denmark, Finland, Germany, Greece, Hungary, Iceland, Israel, Latvia, Netherlands, New Zealand, Norway, Portugal, Romania.

In the UK, legislation prohibiting corporal punishment does not apply to the home or to some alternative care settings.
Source: Global Initiative to End All Corporal Punishment of Children – January 2008

Quotes

'Numerous human rights bodies, including the UN Committee on the Rights of the Child, have made it clear that corporal punishment of children breaches children's fundamental human rights to respect for their dignity and physical integrity. This reality provides an immediate imperative for ending the practice.

'Much work still needs to be done to make Europe a corporal punishment-free zone for children.'
Source: Mieke Schuurman, Secretary General of the European Children's Network, speaking at the launch of the Council of Europe's initiative against corporal punishment of children – Zagreb, June 2008

'Research into the harmful physical and psychological effects of corporal punishment, into the relative significance of links with other forms of violence, in childhood and later life, add further compelling arguments for condemning and ending the practice, suggesting that it is an essential strategy for reducing all forms of violence, in childhood and later life.'
Source: Global Initiative to End All Corporal Punishment of Children – July 2008

⇨ The above information is reprinted with kind permission from politics.co.uk. Visit www.politics.co.uk for more information.

© politics.co.uk

Stop hitting!

Banning all corporal punishment of children

Here are some questions that people often ask about banning corporal punishment...

What is corporal punishment?

'Corporal' means 'physical' – to do with your body. Here, it means 'using physical force to hurt someone or make them uncomfortable'.

'Punishment' means that the force is used to discipline someone – for example, to show them that they have done something wrong, to make them feel sorry, or to teach them how to behave better.

So corporal punishment means punishing someone using physical force in a way which is meant to hurt them or make them uncomfortable. Any punishment using force is corporal punishment, however light it is.

For example, if a toddler spills her drink and her parent hits her on the hand to punish her, that is corporal punishment. Corporal punishment often takes the form of hitting ('smacking' or 'spanking') children.

But it can also take other forms (for example, kicking children, shaking them or forcing them to stay in uncomfortable positions). If a child at school doesn't know the answer to a question and so his teacher forces him to stand on one leg for a long time, that is corporal punishment too.

There are also other forms of punishment which are not physical, but which are just as cruel – for example, making children feel scared or embarrassed on purpose. This kind of punishment is very disrespectful to children and is just as wrong as physical punishment.

Corporal punishment of children can happen in various places – including at home, at school, in other places where children are cared for and in prison.

All kinds of cruel punishment, including all corporal punishment, are wrong and should be banned.

**Global Initiative to
End All Corporal Punishment
of Children**

Does corporal punishment really hurt?

Yes, of course it does! Adults often don't realise that corporal punishment hurts both 'on the outside' and 'on the inside'.

Corporal punishment hurts physically and emotionally, and it can be very humiliating, too. Research on children's feelings and thoughts about corporal punishment is now being done all over the world. In this research, children are telling adults that it does hurt, a lot.

Adults often don't realise that corporal punishment hurts both 'on the outside' and 'on the inside'

The biggest piece of research is *The United Nations Secretary General's Study on Violence Against Children*. In 2006, Professor Paulo Sérgio Pinheiro, who led the study, wrote:

'Throughout the study process, children have consistently expressed the urgent need to stop all this violence. Children testify to the hurt – not only physical, but 'the hurt inside' – which this violence causes them, compounded by adult acceptance, even approval, of it. Governments need to accept that this is indeed an emergency, although it

is not a new emergency. Children have suffered violence at the hands of adults unseen and unheard for centuries. But now that the scale and impact of violence against children is becoming visible, they cannot be kept waiting any longer for the effective protection to which they have an unqualified right.'

Other pieces of research about corporal punishment tell us more about how it can damage individual people and society. For example, a big study published in 2002 showed that children who were physically punished by their parents were more likely to have various problems – including being aggressive and unfriendly, difficulty learning about right and wrong, and mental health problems.

A different piece of research found that two parents out of five who had hit their children had used a different degree of force than they meant to. This means that they might have hit their children much harder than they meant to. Obviously, this could be very dangerous – children, especially babies and small children, could get seriously hurt.

All this research is important. But even if there was no research, corporal punishment would still be wrong. Children have the right to protection from all forms of violence, just as all other people do.

Even if hitting someone doesn't cause them serious long-term damage, it is still wrong to hit them. This is just as true for children as it is for adults.

Most people don't want corporal punishment to be illegal. Shouldn't we listen to them?

No. Children have the right to be protected from violence, even if not everybody agrees.

Governments have to make sure that children's rights are respected. Politicians should do what is right and take a stand on this issue, even if most people don't agree.

In almost all the countries that have

Hitting children is wrong and the law should say so

Information from the Children Are Unbeatable! Alliance

Equal protection from assault for children is a 'matter of priority'

United Nations

The UN Committee on the Rights of the Child, monitoring compliance with the Convention on the Rights of the Child, has recommended equal protection for children to the UK three times – in 1995, 2002 and 2008.

The 2008 report on the UK, published on the 3 October, said: 'The Committee is concerned at the failure of State party to explicitly prohibit all corporal punishment in the home and emphasises its view that the existence of any defence in cases of corporal punishment of children does not comply with the principles and provisions of the Convention, since it would suggest that some forms of corporal punishment are acceptable.'

The 2008 report went on to recommend that the UK should 'prohibit as a matter of priority all corporal punishment in the family, including through the repeal of all legal defences...'

In 2006, the UN Committee on the Rights of the Child reminded all signatories to the Convention on the Rights of the Child, including the UK, that equal protection for children is 'an immediate and unqualified obligation'. The Committee continued: '...the Convention [on the Rights of the Child] requires the removal of any provisions (in statute or common case law) which allow some degree of violence against children (e.g. 'reasonable' or 'moderate' chastisement or correction), in their homes/families or in any other setting.'

The 2006 report of *The United Nations Secretary General's Study on Violence Against Children* called on all countries to prohibit all physical punishment of children by 2009.

Council of Europe

In 2005, the European Committee of

Social Rights, monitoring conformity with the European Social Charter, found UK law in breach of human rights obligations. It concluded: '...since there is no prohibition in legislation of all corporal punishment in the home, the situation [in the UK] is not in conformity with Article 17 of the [Social] Charter.'

Equal protection for children accelerates across Europe

19 countries in Europe – most recently Spain, Portugal and the Netherlands – have now acted to satisfy human rights obligations by giving children equal protection from assault:

2000 Germany; 2003 Iceland; 2004 Romania; 2004 Ukraine; 2005 Hungary; 2006 Greece; 2007 Netherlands; 2007 Portugal; 2007 Spain; 1979 Sweden; 1983 Finland; 1987 Norway; 1989 Austria; 1994 Cyprus; 1996 Italy (by Supreme Court); 1997 Denmark; 1998 Latvia; 1999 Croatia; 2000 Bulgaria.

Of the 47 member states of the Council of Europe, more than half have now legislated for equal protection for children or are committed to doing so soon.

Of the 27 countries of the European Union, only five – one of which is the UK – fail to give children equal protection or have not made a commitment.

'No room for compromise' say UK Children's Commissioners

In their January 2006 joint statement, the four UK Children's Commissioners declared that 'there is no room for compromise' on equal protection for children and called for urgent legislation.

In 2007, Sir Al Aynsley-Green, the Children's Commissioner for England, said: 'Children and young people should have the same right to protection under the law on common assault as that afforded to adults – there is no good reason why children are the only people in the UK who can still be lawfully hit.'

Other bodies that have called for equal protection for children include:

⇨ The independent Commission on the Family and the Wellbeing of Children (2005).

⇨ The National Assembly for Wales (2004).

⇨ The UK Parliamentary Joint Committee on Human Rights (2003).

⇨ The House of Commons Health Select Committee (2003).

Strong professional consensus for equal protection

More than 400 organisations are now part of the Children Are Unbeatable! Alliance which campaigns for the UK to satisfy human rights obligations by modernising the law on assault to give children the same protection that adults take for granted. It is the largest campaign coalition ever formed on a children's issue.

These organisations include:

⇨ All major children's charities – the NSPCC, the National Children's Bureau, NCH, Save the Children and many others.

⇨ All major professional associations concerned with safeguarding children – the British Association of Social Workers, the Royal College of Paediatrics and Child Health, the Association of Directors of Children's Services, the Community Practitioners' and Health Visitors' Association and many others.

⇨ A broad range of faith and church groups, trade unions, sure start projects, children's centres and local safeguarding children boards.

Public consultations evidence supports equal protection

The overwhelming majority of respondents to the Government's consultation on 'reasonable punishment' (section 58 of the Children Act 2004) criticised the current law for being unjust and unsafe. More than 1,000 concerned parents, professionals and organisations submitted evidence to the consultation, conducted in July and August 2007, supporting the case for equal protection for children.

The Government's consultation report, published in October 2007, said:

'Respondents generally felt that section 58 of the Children Act 2004 had made little positive impact on children, families and those working with them. It was considered that section 58 has not improved legal protection for children in cases of alleged assault by their parents. Many respondents felt that the only way to protect children is to ban physical discipline outright.

'Respondents considered that there has been no change in practice as a result of section 58 by those working with children and families in considering incidents involving an alleged assault by a parent upon a child. Most commented that the legal position on the physical punishment of children is confusing for both parents and professionals and makes it difficult to make sound judgements of potential child abuse incidents.

'The general opinion of respondents was that changes to the law have not deterred parents from using unacceptable levels of physical punishment in bringing up their children. A number of respondents were concerned by the use of the phrase "unacceptable levels of physical punishment"; they believed that there is no acceptable level of physical punishment...'

Extract from 'Section 58 of the Children Act 2004 Review (consultation): Analysis of responses to the consultation document', DCSF 2007. October 2008

⇨ The above information is reprinted with kind permission from Children are Unbeatable! Alliance. Visit www.childrenareunbeatable.org.uk for more information.

© *Children are Unbeatable! Alliance*

Record number of adults say smacking children is cruel

Public opposition to smacking is at an all-time high according to new figures released by the NSPCC

The findings come on the day MPs prepare to vote on an amendment to the Children and Young Person's Bill which could finally ban smacking in England and Wales. A total ban would bring England and Wales in line with 18 European countries such as Germany and most recently Spain.

A majority of adults now think it is cruel to smack a child:

⇨ 95% of adults say that smacking a baby under one year old is cruel;

⇨ 73% of adults consider it is cruel to smack a toddler aged one to four. Four is the age when children are most likely to be smacked;

⇨ 54% of people think it is cruel to smack a child of five and older.

The figures are even higher among parents themselves.

NSPCC head of policy and public affairs Diana Sutton said: 'Smacking children is outdated and doesn't work. It's just no longer an acceptable means of discipline.

'It is a national embarrassment that the UK is one of only five remaining EU countries who have not banned or committed themselves to banning the physical punishment of children.

'Public opinion has turned against smacking. It's time politicians listened to the mood of the country and finally make this cruel and antiquated method of punishment illegal.

'This is an opportunity to give children the same legal protection from assault that adults currently enjoy. This may not come again for some time.'

Last Friday, the United Nations Committee on the Rights of the Child criticised the UK Government for failing to prohibit corporal punishment in the family. The Committee said this was a matter of priority.

7 October 2008

⇨ The above information is reprinted with kind permission from the NSPCC. Visit www.nspcc.org.uk for more information.

© *NSPCC*

Defending Government's position on smacking

By the Rt Hon Beverley Hughes MP, Minister for Children, Young People and Families

Some colleagues and children's organisations are arguing that children 'enjoy less protection than prisoners' because parents are allowed to smack their children and that any form of physical punishment, such as a mild smack, is tantamount to an act of violence.

Not only is this not true – as I will explain below – it fails to acknowledge the real problems for families, including children, that a ban on smacking would entail. Let me be clear: we do not encourage or condone smacking and we do not believe that it is the best means of controlling children's behaviour. But neither do we support a ban which would make smacking a crime. If we put a ban on smacking into legislation it would mean in practice that a mother who gives her child a mild smack on the hand when they refuse to put back sweets picked up at the supermarket checkout could end up facing criminal charges.

When we reviewed this issue, as recently as last year, and surveyed parents, we found that while fewer and fewer of them are using smacking as a form of discipline, the majority said they wouldn't support a ban. This reflects the common-sense view that while smacking isn't a good thing, it should not be a crime.

That is why we do not accept any amendment to ban smacking tabled to the Children and Young Persons Bill now going through Parliament.

We are 100% committed to giving children the protection they need. We have already tightened the law to give children greater protection against assault in the Children Act of 2004, which removed the defence of 'reasonable punishment' to any charge of assault occasioning actual bodily harm or worse. Around the same time the bar for a charge of Actual Bodily Harm against a child was lowered because of their extra vulnerability.

This means that parents and carers who cause injuries to their child such as grazes, scratches, abrasions, bruising, swellings and superficial cuts risk being charged with actual bodily harm, which carries a maximum of five years imprisonment. An injury which would lead to a charge of common assault where the victim was an adult, would in most circumstances, if the victim was a child, be charged as actual bodily harm or higher.

Both the Crown Prosecution Service and the Association of Chief Police Officers have said that the law gives them the necessary discretion and power to act in the best interests of the child and the public interest.

But when it comes to smacking, our approach is to provide parents with positive support and guidance to help them manage their children's behaviour more effectively in other ways. That is why we are helping parents access positive parenting courses so they don't resort to physical punishment; why we have established now nearly 3,000 children's centres where parents can get the support and advice they need; why we have promoted and funded parent support programmes in schools, voluntary organisations and local authorities; why every local authority now has a Parents' Champion to promote services and advice to parents and why we have funded the development of more helpline and online advice services to parents.

It is this sort of approach – that works with parents and not against them – that is at the heart of our approach to improving outcomes for children. What the vast majority of parents need is not a change in the law but support and advice so that they can do their very best for their children. In the end, we will only achieve our shared ambitions for children if we bring parents with us.

10 October 2008

⇨ The above information is reprinted with kind permission from the Department for Children, Schools and Families. Visit www.dcsf.gov.uk for more information.

© *Crown copyright*

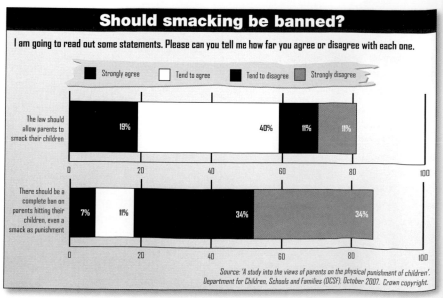

Should smacking be banned?

I am going to read out some statements. Please can you tell me how far you agree or disagree with each one.

Legend: ■ Strongly agree ☐ Tend to agree ■ Tend to disagree ▨ Strongly disagree

The law should allow parents to smack their children: 19% | 40% | 11% | 11%

There should be a complete ban on parents hitting their children, even a smack as punishment: 7% | 11% | 34% | 34%

Source: 'A study into the views of parents on the physical punishment of children'. Department for Children, Schools and Families (DCSF). October 2007. Crown copyright.

banned all corporal punishment, most adults did not agree at first – but once the law was made, many more people changed their minds and began to think that corporal punishment was wrong. In a few years' time, adults will look back and be amazed – and ashamed – that once some people thought it was OK to hit children.

Also, the results of surveys about people's opinions on corporal punishment are not always reliable, because the answers people give can change, depending on how much they know about the subject and how the questions are worded.

Being hit as a child didn't do me any harm. Would I be where I am today if my parents hadn't disciplined me physically?

None of us know how we would have turned out if our parents had never hit or humiliated us.

People who hit children usually do it because they were hit themselves when they were children. There is no point in blaming people in the past for hitting children, because they were just doing what was considered normal then. But times change, and now we know that hitting children is wrong and can be very damaging. Today we realise that children have rights just like everyone else – and it is time to make sure that all their rights are respected, including the right to protection from violence.

Some people say: 'I was hit as a child and I turned out OK.' But there are people who have had all kinds of bad experiences while growing up who have 'turned out OK' as adults – and nobody would say that what they experienced was good. Often it is the way they have dealt with their experiences and turned their lives around that has helped them to be 'OK', not the experiences themselves.

Parents have a right to choose how they bring up their children. Should we interfere even when children are not being abused?

Parents don't own their children – children are people with their own rights.

These rights must be respected everywhere, including at home. Everyone in a family has an equal right to protection from violence, however young or old they are. Just as adults in a family should not hit each other, adults should not hit children – and the law should say so.

The UN Convention on the Rights of the Child says that families are very important. It says that parents have a responsibility to look after children and make sure that they act in their best interests.

Some people say that hitting children to punish them is good for them. But the Committee on the Rights of the Child has said that corporal punishment is never good for children. It is in children's best interests to protect them fully from all forms of violence, including corporal punishment.

Why not tell parents how to hit their children safely, instead of banning all hitting?

There is no such thing as 'safe' hitting. All hitting shows disrespect for children and invades their physical integrity.

Lots of research has shown that often, 'mild' corporal punishment can lead on to much more serious violence against children. Also, adults may sometimes not be able to judge accurately how hard they hit children. See 'Does corporal punishment really hurt?'

A few countries have tried to make laws defining acceptable ways of hitting children, for example by saying that only children of a certain age can be hit, or that children can only be hit in certain ways.

This is a bad thing to do. People would never say that some kinds of violence against women, or against elderly people, are OK. Of course, all violence against these groups of people, and other groups, should be illegal. It is just as wrong to try to say that some kinds of violence against children are OK. Children have a right to equal protection from assault. If anything, children, who are generally smaller and not as strong as adults, have a right to more protection.

But young people sometimes say they don't want corporal punishment to be banned. Shouldn't we listen to them?

Certainly, adults should listen to what children say. But as well as listening, adults should also try to understand children.

Some children and young people do say that corporal punishment is good for them. Adults should listen to these children and young people. But they should also think about why children say this.

Perhaps they don't want to think that their parents would hurt them for no reason. Or perhaps everyone around them thinks that corporal punishment is good, and so they think it is normal.

All children have a right to respect and to be safe from violence. Children everywhere need protection from violence just as much as, or maybe even more than, adults.

In this article, we have already said that through research, lots of children have been telling adults how much

corporal punishment hurts them, physically and emotionally. See 'Does corporal punishment really hurt?'

Many children and young people think that corporal punishment should be banned. In many countries, children are campaigning alongside adults for equal protection from violence.

There is a big difference between beating a child and a loving hit. Isn't banning corporal punishment taking things too far?
No. Beating a child may hurt physically more than a 'loving hit', but they are both violent and they both violate the child's human rights.

When people campaign for an end to violence against women, or against elderly people, they do not say that 'loving hits' should be allowed – they say that all violence against women and elderly people is wrong. So why should it be any different for children?

Talking about 'loving hits' makes it easier for people to seriously hurt children while saying that it is 'for their own good'. Hitting people is not loving behaviour.

Some people say that 'there is a big difference between child abuse and a light hit' – meaning that if a child is not hit very hard, it is less serious. But, however 'lightly' a child is hit, hitting them still violates their right to respect and to physical integrity.

Lawmakers and governments have traditionally said that 'child abuse' and 'corporal punishment' are different things. But most abuse is corporal punishment – many abusive adults use violence on children to punish them and gain control. To protect children and respect their rights, all violence against them should be illegal.

Some people's religions say that they have to use corporal punishment. Wouldn't it be discrimination to stop them using it?
No. People have a right to practise their religion – but they still have to respect other people's human rights.

It's true that some people do believe that their religion tells them to punish their children physically.

However, this does not give them the right to use corporal punishment. People have the right to practise their religion – but only as long as they don't violate other people's rights. All children have the right to protection from violence, whatever religion they or their parents have.

People with very extreme religious views who believe in severe corporal punishment are often disapproved of by other religious people and by society as a whole. Many important religious figures are now joining the campaign to stop all corporal punishment. At the 2006 World Conference of Religions for Peace in Kyoto, Japan, more than 800 faith leaders made 'a religious commitment to combat violence against children'. The leaders came from many religions including Buddhism, Christianity, Hinduism, Jainism, Judaism, Islam, Sikhism, Shintoism, Zoroastrianism and indigenous religions.

In some parts of the world, life is very difficult for many parents, teachers and other people who work with children. Banning corporal punishment will just make life more difficult for them. So shouldn't we wait until things get better before we ban it?
No. Children shouldn't have to wait for protection from violence – they need it now.

This argument clearly shows something that most people already know – often, adults hit children to relieve their own stress or anger, not to teach children how to behave. It is true that many adults all over the world have difficult lives and serious problems – but they should not take these problems out on children.

Adults who lose their temper and hit their children often feel very guilty afterwards. In the long run, banning corporal punishment and using positive discipline instead makes life much less stressful for everyone – both children and adults.

Why do you need to make corporal punishment illegal? Can't you just teach parents not to use it?
Just telling parents that they should not hit their children will not stop them. We need to change the law as well.

The law needs to say clearly that hitting children is wrong. This will send out a clear message to everyone. Then, at the same time as changing the law, governments and other organisations should also teach parents about positive ways of bringing up their children. We need to change the law and offer support to parents.

The idea of making corporal punishment illegal comes from foreign people, not from my country. Corporal punishment is a part of my culture. Isn't trying to make it illegal a type of discrimination?
Hitting children is nothing to be proud of, whoever you are and wherever you come from!

Historically, the tradition of hitting children probably comes mostly from white European cultures.

People from these cultures strongly influenced other countries and brought the idea of corporal punishment with them. Today, the only societies where children are never punished physically are small, hunter-gatherer societies.

Corporal punishment is used in most cultures. All cultures should disown it, just as they have disowned other violations of human rights which were traditional to them. Cultures can change, and people can make choices about how they want their society to be. It doesn't matter where a child comes from, how old they are or what religion they have – all children have the right to protection from violence.

There are movements to end corporal punishment of children now in all continents of the world, and corporal punishment in schools and prisons has been outlawed in many countries all over the world.

Why is it so difficult to give up hitting children?

It is true that lots of adults, including politicians, find the idea of banning corporal punishment very difficult. If they didn't, children would already have equal protection from violence!

There are a few different reasons why adults seem to find it hard to give up hitting children:

1. Personal experience. Most people everywhere were hit by their own parents when they were children.

Most parents have hit their own children. Nobody likes to think bad things about their own parents or about the way they bring up their own children. This makes it difficult for many people to admit that corporal punishment is a bad thing.

There is no point in blaming parents who have used corporal punishment in the past – usually they were just doing what they thought was normal. But now it's time to move on! Corporal punishment should be banned so that children are protected from violence and have their rights respected.

2. Adults often hit children because they are angry, or stressed. When they do this, it can eventually become a habit – so that if the child behaves 'badly', the adult automatically hits them. It is difficult to change habits like this – but it is possible. Parents can choose to bring up their children without violence.

Governments and other organisations, like charities and religious organisations, can help parents to learn about how to do this.

3. Sometimes, parents don't know any other way to teach their children how to behave. But it is possible to learn other ways. Adults and children can live together and have positive, non-violent relationships.

Won't banning corporal punishment mean that children end up spoilt and undisciplined, with no respect for anyone or anything?

No! Children can learn how to behave without violent punishment, through understanding, respect and tolerance.

Corporal punishment does not teach children to respect adults, or help them learn how to behave well. When a child behaves 'well' because they are scared of being punished, they are not showing true respect for adults – they are only showing fear of them. But when parents show respect for their children and discipline them in positive, non-violent ways, children learn to respect their parents in return.

> **Children should be seen as people, whose human rights are just as important as everyone else's. This makes family life better for everyone**

Corporal punishment teaches children that using violence is a good way to solve problems. But positive discipline can help children learn how to solve problems without using violence. Positive discipline doesn't spoil children - it helps them learn to think about how their behaviour affects other people.

Governments should support positive parenting and help parents learn about positive discipline and education without violence. There are lots of materials which can be translated and then used to help parents in any country.

Won't banning corporal punishment lead to children being punished in more horrible ways, such as emotional abuse, humiliation or locking them up?

Children have a right to protection from ALL kinds of cruel punishment and treatment.

As well as corporal punishment, this includes emotional abuse and humiliation (for example, making a child feel upset or embarrassed on purpose). As well as banning corporal punishment, governments should also help parents to learn about positive, non-violent ways of bringing up children.

Parents who hit their children don't feel good about it – they usually feel upset and guilty. Most of them would like to have advice about how to solve problems with their children. Teaching parents about positive parenting helps them to teach their children to understand, accept and respect rules without using any kind of violence, physical or emotional.

We should move on from hitting and humiliating children. Children should be seen as people, whose human rights are just as important as everyone else's. This makes family life better for everyone.

Wouldn't banning corporal punishment mean sending lots of parents to prison and taking their children into care?

No. We don't want to change the law in order to punish lots of parents.

Banning corporal punishment is not about punishing parents - it is about protecting children.

Children should only be taken away from their parents if they are at risk of being seriously hurt. If not, welfare and support services should be offered to the family instead of taking the child away.

In some countries, all corporal punishment has already been banned. There is no evidence from these countries that after corporal punishment was made illegal, more parents were sent to prison. At the moment, it is illegal for adults to hit each other, but an adult who just loses their temper and hits another adult once lightly is very unlikely to go to prison. The same would be true for parents who hit children. But, changing the law would make it easier to punish parents and other adults who do hurt children very seriously.

⇨ The above information is reprinted with kind permission from the Global Initiative to End all Corporal Punishment of Children. Visit www.endcorporalpunishment.org for more information.

© Global Initiative to End all Corporal Punishment of Children

Debate smacks of confusion

The smacking issue

By Stuart Waiton

There are few things that can make the 'tolerant' become intolerant than the mere mention of smacking. Utter the word 'smack', make even a suggestion that it should perhaps not be seen as a form of child abuse, and enlightened, caring, softly-spoken liberals become red-faced with rage. Whether you would personally smack your child or not, this excessive over-reaction suggests that there is something rather strange about the smacking 'debate'.

One or two public figures may 'admit' to having smacked, often with an apologetic tone, but few actively advocate or promote smacking

Speaking at an event in Glasgow last month, I dared to raise the smacking question and suggested that, for parents with small children who misbehave in public, it is hard to know what to do any more as smacking has become such a problematic issue. In the pub afterwards, a social worker told me that if he saw me smacking my children in a supermarket, he would smack me!

As it happens, I was not advocating smacking but merely pointing out that the issue had become overly-confused and problematised. The strange thing is that there is no 'smacking debate' as such. One or two public figures may 'admit' to having smacked, often with an apologetic tone, but few actively advocate or promote smacking. Indeed, rather bizarrely, smacking is associated with being right wing, or at least with being a bit of a Neanderthal. This is all the more peculiar, given the fact that almost 85 per cent of 1,000 adults polled in 2004 agreed that 'parents should sometimes be allowed to smack their children'.

As with many other issues today, what is deemed to be right or the 'correct' way of behaving (the 'tolerant' way) does not actually match the reality of people's lives. The vast majority, it seems, would consider smacking their child, but arguably this same majority would be self-conscious about doing so in front of others. Why is this?

First, we are less of a 'public' today and there are few if any genuine collectively-formed opinions that frame the way issues are understood. Second, in part, because we are more distant from one another, we are also less trusting of other people. The result of this is that, while we may think smacking is OK for us as individuals, we are less sure if we would trust other adults to smack their children.

Most importantly, with the decline of a public voice, experts have filled the vacuum with their own suspicious ideology – an outlook that further encourages a sense of anxiety and doubt among the public.

The issue of 'child abuse' at one level is commonly understood as an extreme act, but this has been confused with the expanding definition given to it by child-care professionals. Today, parents relate to their children, in part, through new expert-constructed 'norms' that have turned the most everyday things, like smacking, into an issue of 'power and abuse'.

Smacking has arguably declined as a form of discipline: with more time on our hands and a more child-focused family arrangement, this is perhaps to be expected, and even a positive thing. Unfortunately, this more 'natural' development of parenting styles is simply confused by the anti-smackers who turn various forms of child discipline into acts of abuse and further help to spread distrust within an already-fragmented society.

Stuart Waiton is director of Generation YouthIssues.org
26 June 2009

⇨ The above information is reprinted with kind permission from the Times Educational Supplement (TES). Visit www.tes.co.uk for more.

© TES

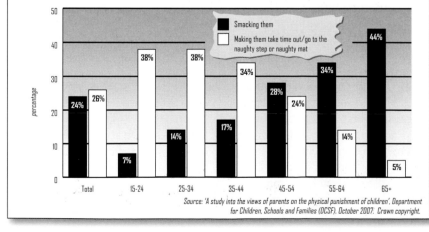

Methods used to manage children's behaviour

Respondents were asked: 'Please think about your child who lives with you/does not live with you and who is ... years old/when your child(ren) aged 18 and over was (were) younger. From this list, which of the following methods of improving your child's behaviour have you used/do you use, if any?'

Legend:
- ■ Smacking them
- □ Making them take time out/go to the naughty step or naughty mat

	Smacking them	Time out/naughty step
Total	24%	26%
15-24	7%	38%
25-34	14%	38%
35-44	17%	34%
45-54	28%	24%
55-64	34%	14%
65+	44%	5%

Source: 'A study into the views of parents on the physical punishment of children', Department for Children, Schools and Families (DCSF). October 2007. Crown copyright.

Shouting at your children as bad as smacking them

By Liz Thomas

At this rate, the only weapon left for parents dealing with extremely difficult children will be a nasty look.

For it seems that shouting at your offspring could follow smacking in falling foul of political correctness.

Parents are now worried that they are letting their children down when they raise their voices to tell them off and fear they could be accused of losing their cool.

Parents are now worried that they are letting their children down when they raise their voices to tell them off

The issue is the subject of a BBC Radio 4 series on parenthood, *Bringing Up Britain*. The first episode will tackle the issue of shouting and disciplining children.

Professor Stephen Scott, of the National Association of Parenting Practitioners, tells the programme that the issue of shouting at children had become an increasing worry.

He added that youngsters needed to experience some shouting in order to prepare themselves for the outside world, where they would meet people who were passionate or emotional.

Professor Scott did warn, however, there was a point when shouting at children became destructive – particularly if it is repeated and personal.

Scientists in the US are starting to look at the impact of verbal abuse alone on young people.

Sue Gerhardt, a psychotherapist who has researched how early experience shapes babies' brains, told the show: 'We can learn from science when parenting. The fact is extreme levels of stress affect the development of young children's brains.

'If you have chronic stress levels – which happens when real fear is generated – over time this will increase the stress hormone cortisol, [which] affects brain development. It is linked with aggression and depression.'

The show's presenter, Mariella Frostrup, said: 'It is increasingly a taboo. I think there is definitely a kind of happy clappy consensus that parents should always talk in measured voices... should never raise their voices, that it is possible to be calm all the time. It's a myth.

'Things have shifted and shifted. In the 1950s – actually even the 1970s – it was fine to give your children a clip around the ear.

'No one is saying we want to return to the days of corporal punishment but now shouting is increasingly frowned upon. I think parents are made to feel very guilty about it.

'We have all seen some harassed parent in the supermarket shouting at an errant child. We probably judge them, and then go home and do the same thing ourselves.'

The 46-year-old is married to human rights lawyer Jason McCue, who is seven years her junior. She came to parenting late, having her first child, Molly Mae, who is now four, aged 41, and then a son, Danny, who is three.

She explained: 'I shout at my kids and then I hate myself for doing it. I know there are far better ways of getting things done, but parents are only human.

'Like many other parents I muddle along feeling hopelessly inadequate most of the time, casting about for advice from any credible quarter along the way.'

Debate about the right to shout has raged on Internet parenting message boards.

One blogger said: 'If you are going to raise a child, you are going to raise your voice sometimes. That is a fact of life.'

Another commented: 'I do raise my voice and shout at my children, and I don't feel guilty. I have had problems for the last year with my now eight-year-old daughter thinking that she can decline to do things I ask her to do.

'When I raise my voice, she knows that I am not kidding and she needs to just do what I said. I usually don't shout until I have said something a few times and been ignored.'

While another said: 'Parents are only human. We should be allowed to demonstrate to our child the whole range of human emotions – that's how he learns about them. As long as the shouting doesn't take over, and the "nicer" emotions are more usual you won't have harmed him.'

The concerns over shouting follow years of wrangling between children's charities, parents and the government over smacking.

It has become an increasing taboo despite the fact that many parents privately believe it is an acceptable way to discipline children.

Under the law, mild smacking is allowed but parents who hit children hard enough to leave a mark face up to five years' imprisonment.

This article first appeared in the Daily Mail, *28 March 2009.*

© 2009 Associated Newspapers Ltd

⇨ Abuse can mean a lot of different things – it's not always easy to know if you or someone you know is being abused. But the important thing to remember is that no-one has the right to hurt you or make you do anything that feels wrong. (page 1)

⇨ When you report child abuse to social services, they must look into it if they think there is a real risk to the safety or well-being of the child. Social services will decide if the child needs protection and what needs to be done to protect them. (page 2)

⇨ In a series of papers published by the *Lancet* medical journal, child abuse experts say that one in ten children in the UK suffers physical, sexual, emotional abuse or neglect. (page 4)

⇨ One in four adults (25%) have been worried that a child they know or who is living in their area is being neglected, and over a third (38%) did not tell anyone about their concerns, a new survey published by Action for Children has revealed. (page 7)

⇨ In the 12 months to 31 March 2008 there were 538,500 referrals of children to social services depart-ments (DCSF 2008). The number of referrals only represents those children identified as 'at risk' of maltreatment and as such is likely to underestimate the number of children being maltreated. (page 11)

⇨ ChildLine counselled more children for sexual abuse in 2007/08 than at any other time in its 22-year history. They included 465 children aged seven or under and nearly 6000 of these calls related to rape. (page 13)

⇨ The Annual Report 2008 from the Internet Watch Foundation (IWF) revealed a fall of nearly 10% in the number of international websites with child sexual abuse content. (page 17)

⇨ Research from Beatbullying indicates that over a third of under-18s have received an offensive or distressing sexual image via text or email. (page 19)

⇨ Statistics from Women's Aid and *Bliss* magazine show that approximately one in five *Bliss* readers have been physically hurt by someone they were dating. The survey also showed that nearly a quarter of 14-year-old girls have been forced to have sex or do something else sexual they didn't want to do by someone they were dating. (page 20)

⇨ At least 10 children have been protected from potential abuse by sex offenders in the first six months of the government's child sexual offender disclosure pilot according to the Home Office. (page 21)

⇨ The vast majority of child abusers have no convictions at all. Criminologist Mark Williams-Thomas estimates there may be as many as 250,000 people in Britain with an active sexual interest in children when only 30,000 have been caught, convicted and signed the sex offender's register. (page 22)

⇨ The majority of sexual offenders are family members or are otherwise known to the child. Sexual abuse by strangers is not nearly as common as sexual abuse by family members. (page 25)

⇨ Every year up to 88,500 sex abuse victims across the UK are left struggling to recover from their ordeal because of a 'postcode lottery' in provision of therapeutic services, the NSPCC has warned. (page 25)

⇨ The first case of False Memory Syndrome in the UK was reported in 1990 and the British False Memory Society was founded three years later. It is now aware of 1,600 families who have been affected by false accusations across Britain. (page 29)

⇨ Studies suggest certain forms of sexual violence against children are on the rise in Europe and that a significant minority of children in Europe, between 10% and 20%, are sexually assaulted during their childhood. (page 29)

⇨ In the UK, legislation prohibiting corporal punishment does not apply to the home or to some alternative care settings. (page 30)

⇨ The 2008 report from the UN Committee on the Rights of the Child recommended that the UK should 'prohibit as a matter of priority all corporal punishment in the family, including through the repeal of all legal defences...' (page 31)

⇨ New figures released by the NSPCC show that a majority of adults now think it is cruel to smack a child: 95% of adults say that smacking a baby under one year old is cruel; 73% of adults consider it is cruel to smack a toddler aged one to four; 54% of people think it is cruel to smack a child of five and older. (page 32)

⇨ A survey from the Department of Children, Schools and Families found that 59% of parents agree that the law should allow parents to smack their children, although a significant minority (22%) disagree and around one in ten parents overall disagree strongly (11%). (page 38)

GLOSSARY

Abuse

Abuse is treating someone with cruelty or violence. Child abuse is when someone is ill-treating a child, causing damage to the child's health or personal development. A child can be suffering abuse if they: have been physically injured; are suffering from sexual abuse; are suffering from emotional abuse, or are being neglected.

Baby P

Peter Connelly, known as 'Baby P', was a 17-month-old boy who died in Haringey, North London, after suffering multiple injuries. Peter was on the Haringey child protection register for physical abuse and neglect during this time. Peter's mother, her boyfriend and his brother were found guilty of causing his death. Baby P's death led to widespread criticism of the social services and an independent review found Haringey's child protection services to be exceptionally 'inadequate'.

Corporal punishment

Corporal punishment refers to the use of physical punishment to correct behaviour. The term comes from the Latin *corpus*, meaning body.

Emotional abuse

Emotional abuse is when someone tries to make you feel bad. This can be saying things on purpose to scare you, or putting you down or humiliating you.

False Memory Syndrome

A controversial theory that, for some adults, repressed memories of childhood sexual abuse that are recovered during psychotherapy may be inaccurate memories and lead to false accusations of sexual abuse.

Neglect

Neglect is when you are not being looked after or supervised properly. If the people who are supposed to look after you don't give you the important things you need, or make it hard for you to take care of yourself, then that's neglect.

Physical abuse

Physical abuse is when someone deliberately hurts or injures you. Hitting, kicking, beating with objects, throwing and shaking are all physical abuse, and can cause pain, cuts, bruising, broken bones and sometimes even death.

Sarah's Law

Following the murder of Sarah Payne by a convicted sex offender in July 2000, Sarah's family called for a scheme under which parents can be told details about anyone who has a conviction for a sexual offence living in their neighbourhood. Under pilot projects launched in some areas in the UK in September 2008, a parent, carer or guardian can request that an individual who has access to their child or children is checked out for a record of child sexual offences.

'Sexting'

Sexting is the act of sending sexually explicit messages or photos electronically, primarily between mobile phones and/or the Internet. Sexting is an extension of cyberbullying when a person (or group of people) deliberately attempts to hurt, upset, threaten or humiliate someone else. This includes when a recipient is made to feel uncomfortable as a direct result of the content, or asked to do something which makes them feel distressed.

Sexual abuse

Sexual abuse is any sexual behaviour between two or more people where there is an imbalance of power. This can include adult/child, older child/younger child, adolescent/younger person, or any situation where one person is forced into participating.

Social networking

A way of interacting with people through sites such as Facebook, Bebo and MySpace. Users can build a profile page containing personal information and photos. To protect yourself online you should be careful what information you give out and who you accept as friends.

INDEX

Additional Resources

Other Issues titles

If you are interested in researching further some of the issues raised in *Tackling Child Abuse* you may like to read the following titles in the **Issues** series:

⇨ Vol. 176 *Health Issues for Young People* (ISBN 978 1 86168 500 1)

⇨ Vol. 167 *Our Human Rights* (ISBN 978 1 86168 471 4)

⇨ Vol. 165 *Bullying Issues* (ISBN 978 1 86168 469 1)

⇨ Vol. 158 *The Internet Revolution* (ISBN 978 1 86168 451 6)

⇨ Vol. 155 *Domestic Abuse* (ISBN 978 1 86168 442 4)

⇨ Vol. 141 *Mental Health* (ISBN 978 1 86168 407 3)

⇨ Vol. 136 *Self-Harm* (ISBN 978 1 86168 388 5)

⇨ Vol. 125 *Understanding Depression* (ISBN 978 1 86168 364 9)

⇨ Vol. 124 *Parenting Issues* (ISBN 978 1 86168 363 2)

⇨ Vol. 99 *Exploited Children* (ISBN 978 1 86168 313 7)

For more information about these titles, visit our website at www.independence.co.uk/publicationslist

Useful organisations

You may find the websites of the following organisations useful for further research:

⇨ **Action for Children:** www.actionforchildren.org.uk

⇨ **Barnado's:** www.barnados.org.uk

⇨ **Beatbullying:** www.beatbullying.org

⇨ **Breathing Space:** www.breathingspacescotland.co.uk

⇨ **Child Exploitation and Online Protection (CEOP) Centre:** www.ceop.police.uk

⇨ **ChildLine:** www.childline.org.uk

⇨ **Children are Unbeatable! Alliance:** www.childrenareunbeatable.org.uk

⇨ **Citizens Advice:** www.adviceguide.org.uk

⇨ **Department for Children, Schools and Families:** www.dcsf.gov.uk

⇨ **Global Initiative to End all Corporal Punishment of Children:** www.endcorporalpunishment.org

⇨ **Home Office:** www.homeoffice.gov.uk

⇨ **Internet Watch Foundation:** www.iwf.org.uk

⇨ **Kidscape:** www.kidscape.org.uk

⇨ **The Lancet:** www.thelancet.com

⇨ **National Institute for Health and Clinical Excellence:** www.nice.org.uk

⇨ **NSPCC:** www.nspcc.org.uk

⇨ **ThinkuKnow:** www.thinkuknow.co.uk

⇨ **Women's Aid:** www.womensaid.org.uk

⇨ **Young Scot:** www.youngscot.org

ACKNOWLEDGEMENTS

The publisher is grateful for permission to reproduce the following material.

While every care has been taken to trace and acknowledge copyright, the publisher tenders its apology for any accidental infringement or where copyright has proved untraceable. The publisher would be pleased to come to a suitable arrangement in any such case with the rightful owner.

Chapter One: Child Abuse

What is child abuse?, © Young Scot, *Child abuse*, © Citizens Advice, *One in ten children suffer abuse, say experts*, © Guardian News & Media Ltd 2008, *Child abuse – signs and symptoms*, © Kidscape, *People 'too afraid' to report child neglect concerns*, © Action for Children, *How the abuse industry is exploiting Baby P*, © Spiked, *Neglected children should be taken from parents*, © Telegraph Media Group Limited (2009), *Guidance to help identify child maltreatment*, © National Institute for Health and Clinical Excellence.

Chapter Two: Sexual Abuse

Counselling for sexual abuse reaches new high, © NSPCC, *Behind every statistic, a young victim*, © CEOP, *Global decrease in child sexual abuse websites*, © Internet Watch Foundation, *Social networking*, © ThinkuKnow, *'Sexting' amongst UK teens*, © Beatbullying, *Teen domestic violence statistics*, © Women's Aid, *Protecting children from sexual abuse*, © Crown copyright is reproduced with the permission of Her Majesty's Stationery Office, *The dangers of Sarah's law*, © New Statesman, *Adult survivors of child abuse*, © Breathing Space, *Abused children 'need therapy'*, © Press Association, *The nightmare of false memories of sexual abuse*, © Guardian News and Media Ltd 2009, *New research sparks fear over paedophile convictions*, ©

Sunday Mercury, *EU steps up fight against trafficking and child abuse*, © European Commission.

Chapter Three: Discipline and Abuse

Corporal punishment, © politics.co.uk, *Hitting children is wrong and the law should say so*, © Children are Unbeatable! Alliance, *Record number of adults say smacking is cruel*, © NSPCC, *Defending Government's position on smacking*, © Crown copyright is reproduced with the permission of Her Majesty's Stationery Office, *Stop hitting!*, © Global Initiative to End all Corporal Punishment of Children, *Debate smacks of confusion*, © TES, *Shouting at your children as bad as smacking them*, © 2009 Associated Newspapers Ltd.

Photographs

Stock Xchng: pages 14 (doriana_s's); 16 (Gabriella Fabbri); 28 (Hazel Brown); 29 (Michal Zacharzewski); 36 (Stacy Braswell); 39 (Thomas Norsted).

Illustrations

Pages 1, 8, 20, 24: Simon Kneebone; pages 4, 12, 22, 26: Angelo Madrid; pages 5, 13, 19, 35: Don Hatcher; pages 10, 31: Bev Aisbett.

Editorial and layout by Claire Owen, on behalf of Independence Educational Publishers.

And with thanks to the team: Mary Chapman, Sandra Dennis, Claire Owen and Jan Sunderland.

Lisa Firth
Cambridge
September 2009